Social skills and personal problem solving

PHILIP PRIESTLEY

JAMES McGUIRE

DAVID FLEGG

VALERIE HEMSLEY

DAVID WELHAM

A HANDBOOK
OF METHODS

TAVISTOCK
PUBLICATIONS

First published in 1978 by
Tavistock Publications Limited
11 New Fetter Lane, London EC4P 4EE
Reprinted 1980 and 1982

Published in the USA by
Tavistock Publications
in association with Methuen, Inc.
733 Third Avenue, New York NY 10017

© 1978 Philip Priestley, James McGuire,
David Flegg, Valerie Hemsley,
David Welham

Phototypeset in V.I.P. Palatino by
Western Printing Services Ltd., Bristol.
Printed in Great Britain at the
University Press, Cambridge

ISBN 0 422 76540 6 (hardback)
ISBN 0 422 76550 3 (paperback)

Our thanks to

Rosemary Barnitt who contributed a lot of the material.

Dr Mary Edwards for help with evaluation methods.

The prison officers who did it first.

Kate Lyon and Martin Seddon for reading it.

Pat Smith for typing some of it.

The Home Office which paid our wages.

More than a thousand other people who have tried out the approach that is described in this book.

Contents

Foreword

This book is divided into three parts. Part One introduces *Social Skills and Personal Problem Solving* and says something about its sources and assumptions. Part Two outlines a four-stage problem-solving process, and describes some of the methods that can be used at each stage. Part Three looks at the construction of programmes, and at applications of the approach and how you can organize it in your own work.

This is also a handbook designed for practical, everyday use. The references to source material have been selected with two main criteria in mind – utility and accessibility – including what we thought to be the most valuable source of each kind, which would be readily available for those wishing to find out more. Where possible, materials and books with ideas for action have been listed; only if there were no alternative source has recourse been made to articles in academic journals. (Also, rather than use the 'op. cit.' convention, we have repeated each reference in full wherever it occurs.)

1 The approach and its origins

1 Social skills and personal problem solving

Social work technique is alive and well and expanding in all directions, into groupwork and encounter, human potential and personal effectiveness methods, the use of behavioural objectives and treatment contracts, task-centred casework, co-counselling, transactional analysis, social skills training, role-play, games, simulations, and many other areas.

But these expanding prospects do not appear to have brought joy to all those who work in the helping agencies. On the contrary, the soul of social work seems to be sick, weighed down from above by a burgeoning bureaucracy and under attack from below by a radical sociology perspective which suggests that it amounts to little more than an insidious and dishonest form of social control. Caught in this dilemma, some workers have made use of the new methods in a piecemeal way in community work, group-work, and, increasingly, in intermediate treatment schemes. Others have sought to elevate welfare rights advocacy into a new orthodoxy almost as narrow as the one it was intended to replace. And others have invested their energies in the pursuit of a professionalism that is somehow above all of these controversies. Mainstream social work has continued to plough a median furrow between using conventional methods, and engaging in those administrative activities that claim an increasing proportion of its time and energy. Meanwhile the manuals of new technique sit on the shelf, their pages largely unturned. And the people on the receiving end, the people with the problems, continue to pay for it all – literally, through their direct and indirect taxes on the one hand and, figuratively, through the receipt of a needlessly second-class service on the other.

This book presents another alternative: a straightforward approach to working with people which combines methods and materials drawn from a wide variety of sources in social work, psychotherapy, education, and training. The aims of the approach are:

1 *to help people solve their immediate problems,*
2 *to improve their ability to cope with future problems,* and
3 *to develop new and increasingly better ways of doing both these things.*

The approach starts from the point at which individuals or groups decide to do something about a problem or problems they face in their everyday lives. But it is not based on professional assessments of what these problems are. It is anchored instead in the experience and perception and personal definitions of the people who have the problems. When people define their own problems in their own way they tend to do so in terms of concrete situations, such as housing, employment, money, and the practical issues that arise from family life, rather than abstract relationships. The approach is concerned, then, with *self-defined problems*.

It is also a *learning* approach, using the word in the broadest possible sense to mean the acquisition and retention for future use of any facts, ideas, or skills that can be used to help solve personal problems of many different kinds. These 'take-away' assets are amongst the most important products of this way of working with people, and they will be stressed throughout the book. They include what have come to be called 'social skills': the ability to manage effectively the exchanges and problems of everyday life. The inability to do this has, in the past, been variously described as moral idiocy, psychopathy, or in less serious cases, simple inadequacy. The imposition of labels like these has acted as a counsel of despair in many instances, indicating the need for coercion or for supportive measures of a more-or-less permanent nature. The idea of social skills is a more hopeful one which suggests that new and better ways of coping with problems can be learned by most people in a manner not too dissimilar from mastering the arts of swimming or riding a bicycle, or operating a centre lathe.

Social skills training does, of course, have strong links with learning theory and behaviourism, but an important feature of the contents of this book is that they have been assembled in a way that is fundamentally *atheoretical*. It owes no allegiance to any particular theoretical perspective on why people are as they are, behave as they do, succeed or fail in life. Nor does it endorse the ideas of any one school of thought about how they can be helped to change. Activities have been included on two grounds: that they make sense to the people who are going to make use of them to solve their own problems; and that they *work*.

But the lack of a 'theory' does not mean that the activities are thrown together without thought; they are structured around three key elements:

1 *Values*: some simple ideas which have grown out of actual experience with these methods. They are essentially humanistic in character and stress the sovereignty of the individuals who take part.

2 *A process*: a framework for action which enables individuals and groups to tackle their personal problems in a systematic but flexible way. The activities are arranged into the four stages of a *problem-solving process* which consists of:

  assessment – finding out what the problem is
  setting objectives – deciding what to do about it
  learning – acquiring the ability to achieve these objectives and
  evaluation – checking up on the results.

3 *Programmes*: written versions of activities from each of these stages which relate to specific problems such as 'finding work', 'handling money', 'accommodation', 'rights', 'violence', and so on, and which together constitute an emerging *curriculum* for the practice of social work.

Together these elements add up to a problem-solving strategy that can be learned by applying it to concrete problems, using some of the tactical skills described in later chapters.

Another principle we have borrowed, and which will become apparent as the book proceeds, is that of *plagiarism*. Workers on the lookout for materials to use in the way proposed here will soon find that the environment is full of them. We advocate the adoption of a 'jackdaw' attitude towards anything at all that may be of value for particular problem-solving programmes. This book is based on the results of our own efforts in this direction over the past few years; much of its content is in common currency and will already be familiar to many readers. All we have done is to rearrange some of it into sequences which may make it more accessible for use in day-to-day work with people with problems.

A curriculum matrix for social work

	Knowing	*Feeling*	*Doing*
Assessment			
Setting objectives			
Learning procedures			
Evaluation			

A device we have also found useful has been the division of problems into three parts: an information or 'knowing' component; an attitudinal or 'feeling' dimension; and a skill or 'doing' aspect. Getting a job for example requires some knowledge of the job market, a basic motivation to work, and the capacity to make successful applications via letters, telephone calls, or interviews. If these *knowing*, *feeling*, and *doing* categories are cross-plotted with the four stages of the problem-solving process (assessment, setting objectives, learning, and evaluation) there is produced a curriculum matrix for the practice of social work, within which it is possible to locate an almost infinite array of methods and materials.

This matrix constitutes what might be described as a 'learning maze' through which individuals or groups can plot their own paths, in their own ways, at their own pace, and towards destinations of their own determining. The rest of the book will concern itself with filling in the blank boxes of the matrix. The overall aims of the book are to:

1 act as a practical handbook which will enable readers to use the approach, or any part of it, in their own work, and
2 illustrate some uses of the approach and suggest others.

The book is aimed in the first place at a wide spectrum of workers in the helping agencies, very broadly defined to cover schools, hospitals, social services, youth work, advisory bureaux, community work, and self-help organizations. Our experience is that, with simple preparation, a very wide range of people are capable of using the approach, or parts of it, to good effect in their work, from the previously untrained and the New Careerist to highly-trained professionals. Clearly it can be done better or worse; and the more time that is devoted to the development of staff skills and course material before starting, the more successful it is likely to be. But in the last resort it is the untrained, the non-professional, and the volunteers who man many of the front-line positions in the war against disease, poverty, inequality, and human distress. It is they who are called upon to do the face-to-face work with people who have problems, and this approach is addressed specifically to their situation. If it gives them the stimulus, the information, and the confidence they need to operate in only a slightly more imaginative and solution-oriented way then it will have succeeded in part of its task. And, as long as the materials and methods are applied in the way we are suggesting, that is, entirely under the control of the people with the problem, then it is unlikely that any of them will do themselves much harm. But if they are seized upon as levers to pry open the problems and secret thoughts of the participants, without their consent or against their better judgement, then little good and not a little damage might be done.

Finally, beyond the agency and the worker, this approach is intended to appeal directly to the people with the problems and to put into their hands the tools they need to dig themselves out of the holes they are in. It aims to equip them with the means of surviving more successfully in complex, urban environments; to communicate effectively, for instance, to make good decisions, to handle difficult social situations, to set and achieve personal goals – to assume, in other words, a measure of control and self-direction over the course of their own lives.

2 Sources and assumptions

Before describing social skills and personal problem solving in more detail, honesty and the laws of copyright demand that some acknowledgement be made of the sources of methods with which this book makes so free. It is difficult to do this adequately without occasionally lapsing into slightly pompous language, as when paying tribute to the importance of rationality and the application of what amounts to a condensed version of 'the scientific method' in this approach. These are common heritages in our culture and it may seem superfluous to mention them, but the growing popularity of anti-rationalist sentiment makes it necessary to stress the straightforward and uncomplicated nature of the procedures described in the following chapters.

Beyond that, the values derive principally from the humanistic tradition in experimental education, psychotherapy, and applied psychology, and the methods mainly from the behavioural tradition of learning theory and training technique.

Sources

EDUCATION

Progressive education and some forms of psychotherapy have contributed the central idea that the child/student/client/patient/group member is the person around whose needs all else should revolve. To this has been added the allied notion of learning by doing, relying on curiosity and self-interest to supply the motive power. 'Freeing the natural child' is the aim of most experiments in education, and their intended end product, like that of this approach, is an integrated, autonomous, and happy human being. But what is missing from the recorded experience of educational innovators such as Froebel, Homer Lane, or A. S. Neill is a set of transportable techniques capable of application by lesser mortals struggling with over-large classes of under-motivated children.

PSYCHOTHERAPY

Classic psychotherapy has suffered much the same handicap, and the rigorous training required for entry into the ranks of the psychoanalysts has ensured its restriction as a treatment to a relative handful of clinical cases. Efforts to overcome these difficulties have led to various translations of the original theory into counselling and casework and, more importantly perhaps, into groupwork. The origins of groupwork are difficult to pin down, but its effects clearly transcend any attempt to see it as little more than a bid to bring therapy to the masses at no extra cost: the presence of others in the therapeutic situation has changed the personal education model of therapy out of all recognition. Amongst other things it has introduced the idea of group members as prime agents in their own therapy, and that of others; one logical extension of this has been the formation of self-help groups such as Alcoholics Anonymous, Synanon, and Gingerbread. Other products of the groupwork movement have assumed less attractive shapes, in which fringe financial and religious interests have become enmeshed. It is not recommended that anyone follow where they have led; but working with groups of individuals who share similar problems, and who can help each other to solve them, is central to social skills and personal problem solving.

LEARNING THEORY

So, from education, some goals have been acquired, together with some related values, and, from psychotherapy, there is a basic format within which to work: the self-help group. But there is still something missing, and that is the activity content which occupies group members in search of solutions to their personal problems. This has been provided by another broad tradition, that of behaviourist learning theories, and its offshoots in clinical psychology and in training for manual and management skills. Now is not the time, and here is not the place, to trace the origins of behaviourist theory; but there are two important lessons to be learned from it. The first is the idea of skills training, in which manual and other tasks are analysed into smaller component parts which can be learned separately and then built back up into the more complex patterns that constitute the practice of the skill in question. This process entails being able to specify in detail the nature of the behavioural learning goal in each case.

The second important feature of behaviourism that has been adopted is the concept of social learning which has replaced earlier, mechanistic models of 'man the learner' with those of a more realistic creature making his way through life by observing and copying the behaviour of others. The processes by which this is achieved are not as yet very well understood, but they make sense as an explanation of much everyday behaviour. And when the idea is combined with that of skill training it produces social skills training. This asserts that complex bits of social behaviour such as complaining or handling aggression can be subjected to analysis in the same way as manual skills, and then reconstructed as training routines for the acquisition of new skills or the enhancement of existing ones. When it works, the result is an extended repertoire of possible responses in situations of stress or personal difficulty. Whether this choice is exercised, and, if so, how, remains at the discretion of the individual, but before he acts his options are that much wider.

THEORY AND PRACTICE

The fact that it has proved possible to combine elements from such divergent traditions is due to a number of historical factors. The most important of them has been the slow but inexorable attenuation of pure theory which has stimulated what amounts to an explosion in methods for use with people in both the therapeutic and the educational fields. As dogma loses its grip on the devotees of a particular school of thought they become free to experiment with the methods developed by workers in other fields. The abandonment of theory has also been accompanied in practice by an erosion of narrow 'professionalism' and a gradual surrender of control to the person on the receiving end of the process. Finally, it is implicit in this surrender, which is still far from complete, that the ends of 'treatment or training' shall be made explicit and subjected to the definitions that individuals make of their own predicament and what they wish to do about it.

The present moment in all these areas is marked by fluidity and innovation, and the convergence of many varieties of thought and action. It is here that the origins of social skills and personal problem solving should be located. And from this ferment of ideas it is possible to distil some values or assumptions which some might wish to describe as the 'theory' of this book.

Theory is a kind of minefield in social work: not too difficult to lay down in the first place; a no-go area for most people who are aware of its existence; and practically impossible to dismantle properly when the need for it has passed. Social work texts tend, therefore, either to avoid the subject altogether, or to gloss over it by assuming that readers share the assumptions of the authors or by effectively concealing the values which lie behind the methods they discuss. If there existed widespread agreement about the proper purposes of social work in our sort of society this failure to make explicit the ideas behind the action would not be too critical. But the increasingly plural nature of the community makes it increasingly necessary to spell out the underlying assumptions of social work so that workers, and the people they are trying to help, can make informed and rational choices about what they are trying to achieve, and why, and how.

Assumptions

COMMON SENSE

The approach presented in this book can lay claim to neither an elaborate value system, nor an elegant theoretical position, but it does rest on a modest set of working assumptions which give shape to its activities and a recognizable style to the way it looks and feels in practice. It is the purpose of this chapter to set out these values as simply and fully as possible so that the reader can test them against his own and judge their relevance to his own area of work. The assumptions themselves acknowledge only one real debt, and that is to everyday rationality or common sense. Added together they could be said to constitute a 'view of man', but it is one that falls well short of the rigour and logical connectedness required of a full-blown theory. In a word, our 'view of man' is an educational one rather than a medical one. We do not assume that people are sick or in need of treatment. We assume instead that most people would like to learn how to cope with some of the situations in their lives in ways that are more effective or more congenial to themselves and others. And, unlike 'treatment', learning is a morally neutral activity which implies no stigma for those who engage in it.

Looking at personal problems and learning how to cope with them better are the twin hinges on which the whole of the enterprise turns. Much the same is claimed by supporters of other approaches; what is distinctive about personal problem solving is the way it combines methods and materials drawn from the most catholic array of sources into coherent sequences or programmes. Ironically, it is the denial of formal theory that not only permits but positively stimulates this 'gleaning' orientation to the products of other schools. But it is common sense that informs their rearrangement into the simple logic of a four-stage problem-solving process consisting of assessment, setting objectives, learning, and evaluation. At its least ambitious the use of the process is intended to secure some progress, however slight, towards the solution of some personal problem, no matter how trivial it may appear. At its most ambitious it is concerned with the attainment of personal autonomy by all possible means.

SELF-DEFINED PROBLEMS

Movement towards goals of any kind must start with an awareness of some personal problem and a desire to do something about it. People are hardly ever motivated to solve problems that have been defined for them by others. It is essential, therefore, that the problems to be dealt with should be ones as seen and expressed by the individuals who have them. When people are asked to say what their own problems are, they often locate them outside themselves as tangible puzzles or in actual patterns of behaviour: getting a job, for instance, or a place to live, or dealing with debts, or drink, or noisy neighbours. They do not naturally think in terms of abstractions such as 'relationships', or 'guilt', or 'authority'. This lack of coincidence with the aims of social work agencies and with the trained judgements of their professional employees may make the tackling of such problems unattractive to some. But the self-definition of problems is vital in producing the level of motivation necessary for effective learning. Looking at one's own life in this way, like looking in a mirror, appears to hold a perennial fascination for many human beings. And this unfailing source of curiosity and energy can be harnessed to the learning efforts of all sorts and conditions of men, including many who have proved immune to the more conventional ministrations of social work. It should also be emphasized that, when left to themselves, people do not, as some social workers might fear, define fantasy problems and even more fantastic solutions to them. When dealing with social workers and other officials, lies and concealment may represent the most rewarding or the least damaging strategy an individual can pursue. For the individual engaged in solving some self-defined personal problem, such behaviour would serve no useful purpose.

The worker may, of course, disagree about the relative importance of the problems being worked on, and may even think that fundamental personal issues are being ignored. He is entitled to his opinion, and he may or may not be right, but it is not his job in a problem-solving exercise to impose his interpretations on others, no matter how skilfully or gently he may do it. He is there to provide the resources that will permit individuals and groups to come to their own conclusions, in their own way and in their own time, about the problems they say they have.

VOLUNTARISM

Learning is, of course, possible without consent, as in operant conditioning and brainwashing. But learning is likely to last longer and to take deeper root when the learner concerned has freely chosen to co-operate in the proceedings, has formulated his own learning goals, is free to select the means of achieving them, and pursues them in an orderly, self-conscious, and willing way. Voluntary participation is in fact the linchpin of the assumptions set out in this chapter. Participants in a problem-solving exercise must be free to join or not to join in the first place, free to stay or leave at any time subsequently, free to accept or reject any activity which is on offer, and free to make whatever use they deem fit of the results of any of the exercises they choose to complete. Such a degree of freedom may appear to be utopian and unattainable, and even somewhat frightening, to those whose vision is constrained by the more authoritarian forms of learning which are common in our society, e.g. compulsory school attendance backed by legal sanctions and the threat of force; corporal punishment; the discipline of the exam syllabus; and even the invisible tyranny of unthinking deference to rank or custom or socially-sanctioned expertise. In practice this freedom works. It works by creating an atmosphere of consent and co-operation which facilitates and intensifies whatever learning is undertaken. And it is rarely abused, in our experience at least, by any capricious picking and choosing for its own sake. Once trust has been established, and the reality of free choice has been experienced, there develops an open-minded willingness to try most things and to assess their personal utility afterwards. This atmosphere does not need to be built up in any special way; it seems to grow naturally out of the application of the principles outlined in this chapter, and of the practical activities described in later chapters. It appears to be what happens spontaneously when people work together, without external constraints, towards mutually agreed ends.

It could be argued that an insistence on voluntary participation rules out the use of the approach in a wide variety of situations and settings where consent is not now, and never will be, the order of the day: in prisons, for example, mental hospitals, community homes, and supervision under court orders. The argument has some validity in that it would never be possible to organize the whole of the regimes in some of these places along the lines being proposed here. But there is no reason why short-term, voluntary learning exercises should not be organized and successfully concluded in even the most unfree environment. We have found in prisons that it is perfectly possible to create self-contained islands of choice and co-operation where the ordinary rules and disciplines of the institution are inoperative. That does not mean that there are no problems to working in this way in those kinds of places (just the opposite is true), but it *is* possible. It could also be argued that the principle of voluntarism excludes from the reckoning a large number of people who could benefit mightily from the method, but whose problems are ones that they do not, or cannot, or choose not to admit either to themselves or to others. That is true, but it is not the purpose of this approach to cajole or coerce anyone into acquiring insight into his own shortcomings as seen by others. There are, after all, enough people in the world with sufficient awareness of their difficulties and the will to do something about them voluntarily to keep all known social workers, mental health staff, counsellors, youth leaders, and voluntary agencies busy for several lifetimes. The unaware may still pose a problem or a threat to those around them, but they are candidates for social control and not for voluntary learning.

VARIETY AND CHOICE

Choice in learning has two further preconditions: one is a range of things from which to choose; and the second is a clear appreciation of the nature of the alternatives. There is no shortage of things to do, as subsequent chapters will show, but multiplicity of methods is not something that should be approached in the spirit of an undiscerning stamp collector. The need for variety arises simply from the fact that different people learn about different things in very different ways. And, since there is no way of knowing in advance who is going to learn what from which activity and how, it is necessary to provide as many routes as possible to the same learning goals. Learning is not just something that takes place in narrowly defined circumstances, although the idea of desks and blackboards dies hard. A problem-solving programme of the kind outlined in this book may contain activities as varied as filling in forms and tests, conducting street interviews with a video-tape recorder, rehearsing dating behaviour, preparing and delivering a talk on some aspect of work or leisure, watching films, or engaging in group discussion or interviews with fellow group members. One individual may be deeply engaged by a particular activity; another may be bored by it. Both may get something or nothing from the discussion that follows. The process may be repeated but in reverse during the next session of the programme. At the conclusion of a complete programme each member of a group is likely to have learned something, but by an itinerary that is unique to himself.

EXPLICITNESS

In order to decide whether to sample any or all of these learning activities a participant will need to have their aims and methods spelled out clearly to him. Explicitness is necessary at every stage if realistic choices and decisions are to be made. This can create difficulties for programme organizers. If an activity cannot be described in such a way that even the non-literate and the less than intellectually gifted can recognize and respond to its potential helpfulness, then, whatever its merits in the eyes of the workers, it should be omitted from the programme. 'If you can't explain it; don't do it,' is the simple but brutal rule dictated by the principle of explicitness. This is not intended to condemn things excluded in this way as pointless or useless; they may well be neither. But it does emphasize the sovereignty of the user in this approach. Everything that happens must be submitted to the double test of everyday comprehensibility, on the one hand, and of consumer acceptability, on the other.

OPENNESS

Explicitness of purpose and process is intimately linked with a further principle, one of rather looser texture: that of 'openness'. The first casualty of openness in the context of personal problem solving is the conventional interpretation of the idea of 'confidentiality'. This typically consists of keeping files full of information to which the 'client' is not allowed access. Information is the lifeblood of problem solving; it is the raw material from which decisions about problems have to be fashioned. It would not make much sense, therefore, to collect information which was then concealed from the person most concerned, namely its contributor. Whenever information is generated by someone about a personal problem, it is his to keep in a personal file, and his to share or not with others as he chooses. The information is about him and his difficulties; his only purpose in collecting it is to help solve a particular problem. The copyright is his, and any use of the data, besides that to which he gives his consent, is illegitimate. In practice most people are willing to divulge most of the data in their files to other members of their group, but their right not to do so must be made clear from the start. The same principle extends to contacts between staff members and third parties. Within the problem-solving framework these would never take place without the agreement of the participant and should be conducted in his presence or, in the case of telephone calls, his hearing. Social workers should also resist the temptation to take bits of evidence from a problem-solving experience in order to strengthen or deepen their official case notes. And, finally, openness refers to the whole style of the operation. It is one in which everything is explicit and superficial in the best sense of the word. There is nothing up anybody's sleeve, no secret agenda, no hidden depths, no mystifying theories, no 'eclectically esoteric jargonification', and no activities that mean anything more than can be seen with the naked eye.

EQUALITY

It follows from the nature of these assumptions that the relationships which are created between the people involved will not normally correspond to those of leaders and led, teachers and taught, workers and clients. Both the providers and the consumers of a problem-solving programme find themselves in what amounts to a shared learning situation. The participant is learning about his problem and how to tackle it. The organizer is learning how to run ever-improving programmes, how to devise more and better materials, how to present them more effectively, and how to tailor them more closely to the needs of particular groups and individuals within them. His role in all this can be likened to that of an engineer who is employed to hand tools to a 'do-it-yourself' operative, explaining how they work, offering them in the right order and at the right time, and helping to look critically but constructively at the finished product, but leaving all the doing to the person with the problem. Or, like the artist's apprentice, he prepares the canvas and the colours and watches while the master paints the picture. This 'fitter's mate' style of relationship may not appeal too much to those with a heavily 'professional' view of the social worker's role, but the analogy is meant to be suggestive rather than definitive. The most important points to be made about what the organizer does are: first, that he acts as a kind of broker between people and their problems on the one hand and learning opportunities on the other; and, second, that he should perform this task with affection and respect for the people who patronize his efforts. This definition of the staff role is not put forward for any doctrinaire reasons; it is the practical outcome of concrete experience with large numbers of people in a variety of places. We have found that when people work together on an equal footing, each with their distinctive contribution to make to the common task, they not only find it congenial in an unforced first-name kind of way, they also seem to get the job done quicker and better.

OPTIMISM AND CHEERFULNESS

Two final expectations contribute to the atmosphere that permeates successful problem-solving exercises: optimism and cheerfulness. Optimism implies that individuals are far more capable of changing and growing, and learning and influencing their environment, than either they or others ever imagine. It asserts, in short, that most people possess unused capabilities which can be mobilized to increase personal competence, both in the ordinary events of everyday life and in some of the extraordinary crises that arise from time to time. This optimism is not naive and it is not sentimental; it is solidly rooted in practical experience. It is a fact of common observation that most human beings have the capacity to learn far more than they already know and to acquire skills quite outside their ordinary repertoire. And, because people respond to the benign contagion of positive expectations, an atmosphere of optimism is one that will help produce better results. In practical terms this means looking for strengths, as well as weaknesses, and providing positive reinforcement for the successes of group members.

Strictly speaking, good humour and cheerfulness do not qualify as values of the kind we have been discussing; nor do they feature prominently in many social work primers. We entertain a strong expectation that most people will find problem solving an enjoyable experience. The enjoyment is not an end in itself, and the expectation is not held with grim 'holiday-camp' determination. But, contrary to the beliefs of what may be called the 'growth is pain' school, we have found that successful learning is a profoundly liberating experience; and its natural accompaniments are exhilaration and laughter.

Notes and references

The nature of this book makes it virtually impossible to document properly. The number of references to the work of others could fill a volume as big as the text itself. The notes which follow are intended, therefore, to be indicative rather than exhaustive, the books referred to acting as guides to the wider literature of which they are a small part.

It would be pointless, for instance, to say much about 'the scientific method' or do much more about it than refer interested readers to works such as J. R. Ravetz (1971) *Scientific Knowledge and its Social Problems* (Oxford: Oxford University Press), or M. Polanyi (1958) *Personal Knowledge* (London: Routledge and Kegan Paul).

Nor is there any neat way of summarizing the places and sources from which ideas have been taken to form the substance of this account. A good introduction to the general spirit of the proceedings would be C. Rogers (1969) *Freedom to Learn* (Columbus, Ohio: Merrill). (Incidentally, we did not come across this example of ideas that are 'in the air' until our book was already written.)

Similarly, in education it would be possible to start with classics such as Rousseau's *Emile* or Froebel's *Education of Man* and to suggest a course of reading amongst the works of Dewey, Annie Besant, Bertrand Russell, Francisco Ferrer, and Susan Isaacs. But A. S. Neill (1968) *Summerhill* and P. Goodman (1971) *Compulsory Miseducation* (Harmondsworth: Penguin) are more recent and more accessible representatives of this general tradition in education. And D. Wills, besides applying the principles in his own work – see (1945) *The Barns Experiment* (London: George Allen and Unwin) – has written a biography of *Homer Lane* (1964; London: George Allen and Unwin).

The development and uses of groups in psychotherapy are equally difficult to trace: M. Jones (1968) *Social Psychiatry in Practice* (Harmondsworth: Penguin) is a good introduction to therapeutic communities. Other useful titles include N. Walker (1957) *A Short History of Psychotherapy* (London: Routledge and Kegan Paul) and R. J. Corsini (1957) *Methods of Group Psychotherapy* (New York: McGraw-Hill).

For learning theory, a comprehensive review is provided in F. H. Kanfer and J. S. Phillips (1970) *Learning Foundations of Behavior Therapy* (New York: Wiley). A. Bandura's writing is of considerable importance in this field, e.g. (1963) *Social Learning and Personality Development* (New York: Holt, Rhinehart and Winston). And D. Jehu (1967) *Learning Theory and Social Work* (London: Routledge and Kegan Paul) reports some earlier adaptations of learning theory to personal problems.

The relevance of cognitive psychology to behavioural ways of working with people is illustrated in D. Meichenbaum (1977) *Cognitive Behavior Modification: An Integrative Approach* (New York: Plenum).

2   A problem-solving process

3 A problem-solving process

3 Assessment

If you want to solve a problem, the first thing you need is as much information as possible about it. There are those who arrive at solutions by leaps of intuition and imagination; but more pedestrian folk have to rely on rather more predictable ways of getting results. This chapter describes a number of practical assessment techniques which can be used by individuals or groups.

The aims of assessment

Assessment is the first of the four stages of the problem-solving process, which occupies the next four chapters; and the term embraces any activity whatsoever that generates information that can be used to find solutions to personal problems. It does not mean a clinically detached process of observation and classification by 'experts'. Although many of the procedures derive from the work of theorists, academics, and professionals, we recommend that they be handed over wholesale to the consumers to be used, as they see fit, in what is essentially a process of *self-assessment*.

More precisely, the purposes of assessment are:

1 to define and describe personal problems in as much detail as possible;
2 to catalogue personal strengths as well as weaknesses. Dwelling on defects to the exclusion of all else will help no-one solve a problem. Assessment should also identify 'positives' around which solutions can be constructed;
3 to teach 'take-away' assessment skills for use with future problems. The whole emphasis of this approach is on learning how to cope better with problems, not just on one occasion but permanently;

4 to collect the information required for the next stage of the process, that of setting personal objectives. It sometimes happens that assessment by itself will produce the answer, but it is more often the case that it will provide the raw materials for deciding what to do next.

MAKING A START

Before actually embarking on any assessment activities, it is essential to spend some time explaining to participants the aims of this part of the problem-solving process. These might be based on the purposes just listed, but with changes and additions relevant to particular circumstances. But, whatever they happen to be, they should be written on a large sheet of paper and displayed prominently throughout the proceedings to which they refer.

Some thought and discussion should also be devoted to the question of control over the results of assessment. Our own view is that they belong to the participant, and should be kept by him in a personal file to which access can only be gained with his express permission. This does not normally lead to excessive secrecy or the unnecessary withholding of vital data, but it does contribute to the creation of an atmosphere in which participants feel in charge of what is happening. And it appears to lead in turn to a greater degree of self-disclosure. The rules about these and other matters will clearly vary from place to place and from time to time, but they should always be made explicit and written down, either in the form of a hand-out for distribution to group members or on a wall sheet, so that there can be no misunderstanding about the conduct of the assessment procedures.

Some agreed rules for assessment

1 All assessment exercises are *voluntary*. If you think some part of the assessment is not relevant to you, or you dislike it for any other reason, do not do it.

2 The results of any pencil-and-paper test, interview, or other activity belong to you. You need not show them to anyone else, unless you wish to; you can destroy anything you are not happy with; and all the information is yours to take with you at any time.

3 Staff members will not reveal to anyone else anything they learn during assessment sessions without the permission of the person involved.

What is the problem?

Although individuals or groups are likely to become involved in problem solving because they have acknowledged a specific difficulty, it is still a good idea to start the assessment stage by asking them to say in their own words what they think their problem is.

SENTENCE COMPLETION

Some diagnostic methods approach this delicate subject in an oblique and indirect fashion, but we have found that one of the simplest and most effective ways of getting quickly to the heart of the matter is to invite people to complete the sentence:

My biggest problem is ....

The response can obviously be made inside someone's head, or by telling another person, or, most usually, by writing down the complete sentence on a piece of paper. Further problems may be elicited by completing a further sentence:

I also have problems with ....

It may be objected that replies to these 'naive' questions will be shallow and misleading, which is clearly sometimes the case. But when people have real problems and are concerned to do something about them, and have consented to take part in a problem-solving process, their answers are, more often than not, a blunt expression of what is bothering them.

Another straightforward way of obtaining a first statement of problems is that of 'brainstorming'.

BRAINSTORMING

This is a widely-used method for helping groups to produce large quantities of ideas. It fits into any stage of the problem-solving process but it is particularly useful during assessment for creating lists of concerns, and for exploring the endless web of feelings that seem to surround many personal difficulties.

All that is needed for brainstorming is a blackboard, or a large sheet of paper on a wall, and something to write with.

Explain to the group that the aim of a brainstorming session is to generate as many ideas as possible on a given topic. The basic rules of the exercise are:

1 suspend judgement – the value of the ideas can be sorted out later;
2 aim for quantity not quality;
3 let the mind wander – wild and quirky ideas can turn out to be winners;

PATIENTS' PROBLEMS

APATHY   DRINK   MONEY

                            WORK

CONCENTRATION MOTHERS CONFUSION

INTOLERANCE DRUGS SEPARATING

GETTING UP HOSPITAL SELF-RESPECT

INCENTIVE FEELING UNCERTAINTY

FEAR   AGGRESSION DISHONESTY

ANGER   ESCAPING

                    INEXPERIENCE

PLEASURE EMOTION

                    NOISE

CIGARETTES UNDERPRIVILEGED

MATCHES   LOVE TOLERANCE

FIRE   ISOLATION

  INDIVIDUALITY INSIGHT COMMUNITY

  FAMILIES   NEGLECT

  COMMUNICATION HOPE LACK OF
                          PAST

              CARE

4 build on the ideas of others – respond to what is already written up, add to it,
   expand it.

The title of the topic or problem is written at the top of the sheet and group
members call out the ideas that occur to them and these are written up as quickly
as possible, which usually means as one-word abbreviations. In the example on
page 24 a group of workers in a psychiatric hospital were asked to brainstorm *patients'
problems.*

When a sheet, or several, have been filled in this way (the one shown took less than
five minutes) the contents may be sorted out into smaller lists of related ideas around
which programme activities can be planned.

Emotional states	*Behaviour*	*Addictions*
apathy	getting up	drink
intolerance	matches/fire	drugs
fear	dishonesty	cigarettes
anger	aggression	
pleasure	work	
feeling	money	
emotion		
love		
uncertainty		
confusion	*Other people*	*Self*
hope	families	individuality
	mothers	isolation
	community	insight
	separating	self respect
	communication	lack of past
		inexperience

The results of a brainstorm like this are rough and ready, but they do represent a
snapshot of a group's concerns, and can act as a provisional agenda for the activities
that follow. But because of the public nature of the method and the natural reticence of
newly met group members, the output of a single brainstorm should not be regarded
as definitive. A re-run of the exercise at a later point in the life of the group could well
produce substantially different ideas, so more private methods should be used at the
same time.

CHECK LISTS

One way of doing this is with a problem check list, of which several examples are in widespread use; the best known of them is probably the Mooney Problem Checklist. This contains 146 items covering such areas as work, money, being in trouble, health and appearance, social life, personality, home, and family, and it leaves space for users to add categories of their own. It is not too difficult for staff members to compile their own check lists along these lines, and to present them in something like the following form:

A problem check list

	Often a problem	Sometimes a problem	Never a problem
I worry about my appearance		✓	
I think there is something wrong with my heart			✓
I haven't got any friends		✓	
I never do as I'm told	✓		
I need to save more money	✓		
People criticize me a lot		✓	

The person filling in this type of check list is asked to indicate with a tick whether a particular statement applies to him and, if so, with what degree of frequency.

CARD SORTS

An active alternative to check lists and some other questionnaires is the card sort. Instead of listing the items on a piece of paper, each statement or question is typed onto a separate card. The complete pack is then given to an individual who is asked to sort the cards into different piles. General problem items, for example, could be sorted into three separate piles: 'severe problem', 'a problem', and 'not a problem'.

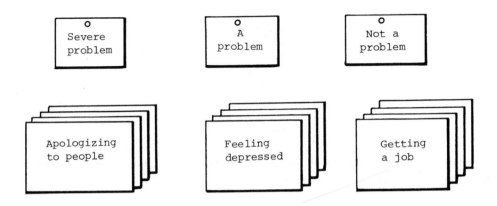

Any or all of these methods for procuring a first statement of problem areas should be accompanied by group discussion. Even the most general discussion will spark off fresh ideas and thoughts in people's minds. It also stimulates introspection, one of the first signs that real problem solving is beginning to take place. It may take a session or two, but after a while some group members will complain that their 'brains are hurting' or their 'heads are going round and round'. This usually means that they are doing some unaccustomed thinking about themselves and their lives. And the capacity to do that is the first of the 'take-away' skills with which this approach seeks to equip its participants.

These preliminaries need not take long to complete, but if they are successful they will have generated a list of topics around which the remainder of the exercise can be built. But, at this stage, they are unlikely to consist of much more than single-word labels to situations which often conceal a many faceted complexity. Assessment must therefore look more closely at the personal meanings behind these labels.

Analysing problems

One of the reasons why some personal problems remain untackled is because they look too big or too difficult to their owners. One of the tasks of assessment is to help them break down these large and unmanageable problems into smaller and less intimidating parts, and to acquire this analytic ability for future use.

THE '5W–H' SYSTEM

One way of doing this is to use the '5W–H' system, which consists of asking, in relation to any problem, the questions:

> What?
> Who?
> Where?
> When?
> Why
> *and*
> How?

Someone with severely limited confidence in social situations might answer these questions in this way:

What is the problem? — Meeting new people and making conversation with them.

Who does it affect? — Me, mostly; my wife, who finds it difficult to lead a normal social life because I am so shy; and some of the people I can't avoid meeting, who must think I am being deliberately rude to them.

Where does it happen? — Almost everywhere, although I avoid some of the worst places like pubs and clubs.

When? — Usually when I am least expecting it; like when we go to the supermarket and bump into someone my wife knows from her work.

Why? — I am just naturally shy; I blush when I meet people I know quite well.

How could it be tackled? — Don't really know. I am quite good on the telephone; perhaps I could build on that.

PATTERN NOTES

Pattern notes are another useful tool for elaborating brief descriptions of problems and problem areas at this stage of assessment. They are described by Tony Buzan in the BBC publication *Use Your Head*. According to Buzan, making notes in straight lines across and down the page is quite alien to natural thought processes. He advocates instead starting with the title, which might be 'drink', or 'drugs', or 'sex', in the centre of a sheet of paper, and developing ideas along lines or dividing branches radiating out from it, with new branches for major sub-branches and connections between related areas. For example, someone with a drink problem would write the word 'alcohol' in the middle of the page and develop pattern notes around it.

Most people are able to write productive pattern notes after only one demonstra-

Problems of the long-term prisoner

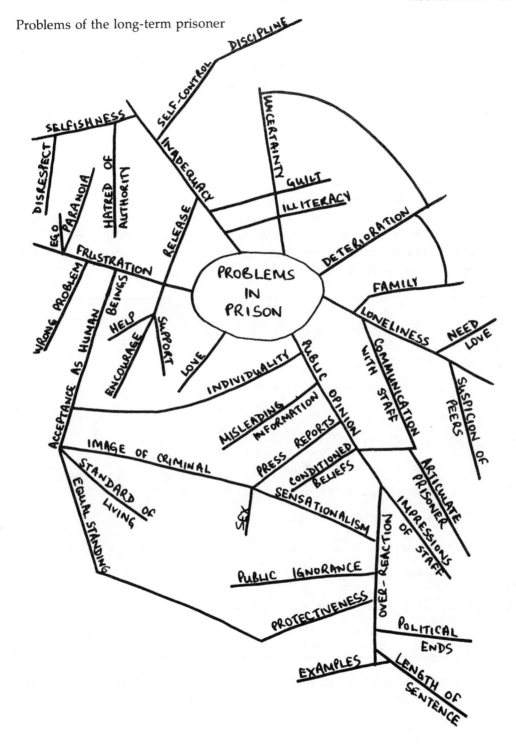

tion of the method, but others need a little practice at it. Pattern notes can also be written on a group basis, quickly evoking a rudimentary map of members' ideas, concerns, and constructs. And for those people who find them congenial they are a perfect example of a 'take-away' skill which can be used over and over again. In the example on page 29 a group of long-sentence prisoners were producing ideas on the problems they faced in prison.

RANKING

Ranking can help to make sense of multiple problems, or of specific parts of particular ones, by putting them in order of importance, urgency, or difficulty. Most people will have seen the method on their cornflakes packet in competitions where you can win a car by ranking some of its features in order of desirability. Adapted to assessment, ranking will indicate priorities amongst a set of personal problems or, as in this example, the constituent elements of a decision.

Choosing a job

_____ Pay

_____ Holidays

_____ Training opportunities

_____ Working hours

_____ Fringe benefits

_____ Physical working conditions

_____ Interesting work

_____ Opportunities for advancement

_____ Social life

_____ Distance between work and home

Look at the above list and choose the item which is most important
to you in selecting a job, indicating your choice with the number 1.
Write number 2 against the next most important item, number 3 against
the next, and so on, until you have completed the list.

Apart from these simple methods for expanding and elucidating the problems people define for themselves, other points of entry into them may be opened up by asking and seeking answers to questions about 'self' such as 'what sort of person am I?', 'how do other people see me?', and 'what are my strengths and weaknesses?'. Or the dimension of time may repay closer attention, scrutinizing personal experience in an organized fashion, tracing the natural history of a problem, and even treating time, its uses and abuses, as something worth assessing in its own right.

Smaller bits of bigger problems can also be broken off by making use of the *knowing*, *feeling*, and *doing* classification introduced in the first chapter of this book.

Knowing refers to the quantity and quality of information held by an individual about his problem and the ways in which it might be solved to his own satisfaction. This could include the kind of personal knowledge sometimes called 'insight', but it is based more broadly than that. Some difficulties are due entirely to ignorance, as when someone does not know of his entitlement to a cash grant for some purpose. The solution is to give him this information directly, or to create the opportunity for him to acquire it for himself. The amount of knowledge in someone's possession, its accuracy, and relevance, can be assessed in a variety of ways.

But sometimes it is not just a question of ignorance. An elderly lady may be well aware that she can claim a special heating allowance from the DHSS but be too proud to ask for it. What prevents her from claiming it is the nature of her attitudes or *feelings* towards 'The Assistance'. It is helpful therefore to assess *how* people *feel* about the problems in which they are enmeshed, in case it provides clues to possible solutions. In the case of the elderly lady, it could lead to attempts to change her attitudes by inviting her to talk to other elderly ladies who make similar claims without undue feelings of shame or dependency. Feelings can be investigated by various methods.

Yet another person may *know* all that is necessary to solve a problem, and be *well-motivated* to tackle it, and yet still lack the skills required to put it into practice. He should therefore concentrate on the *doing* aspects of his difficulties. These can range from the simplest function such as buttoning up an overcoat to the most complex such as mediating in a long-standing family feud. In between these two extremes there are a host of practical, occupational, intellectual, and social skills which it is possible to acquire. Finding out how well people do things is thus another vital part of assessment.

In the rest of this chapter, some examples of assessment methods for looking at these and related areas will be described in detail, followed by a look at the methods themselves and some suggestions about their use in practice.

Looking at self

A lot of the people who end up on the files of the helping agencies have grown accustomed to submitting themselves to the scrutiny of a succession of workers. But the idea of looking at themselves in a systematic way is not one that would normally occur to them spontaneously; nor is it likely that they would respond to invitations to dwell before their reflections in some of the muddier backwaters of the personal growth movement. But many of them will react positively to straightforward and self-evidently useful methods for looking at themselves constructively, and it is one of the purposes of assessment to provide a variety of opportunities for doing this.

Sentence completion is one of the most obvious places to begin. Completing the sentence:

I am ....
I am ....
I am ....
I am ....

several times will create, in a short space of time and with very little effort, an interesting self-portrait, couched entirely in the language of the person concerned. It may contain strengths and weaknesses in varying proportions. It may be glowingly self-congratulatory. More often it will be negative in tone, in which case the individual should be encouraged to complete the sentence a few more times, but more optimistically. It is also interesting to continue the exercise until the participants have run out of things to say about themselves. This will happen surprisingly quickly in many instances; but if the process is repeated later in a problem-solving experience it is possible to discover whether someone has developed a more detailed and interesting view of himself.

SELF-PERCEPTION SCALES

Rating scales are a slightly more formal method of achieving similar results. These may be verbal, or they may be numerical scales like this one:

Rate yourself on the following scale:

Kind 3 2 1 0 1 2 3 Unkind

Put a ring round the number which is nearest to where you think you are on the scale.

If several scales using pairs of opposite adjectives are put together they form an interesting self-perception exercise.

In the example below the scales have been completed twice: once for 'me as I am' and once for 'me as I would like to be'. These should be done on separate sheets first and then combined so that the gaps between the two profiles become immediately obvious. On those items where the gaps are large ones, a target for action is opened up at once. The person who filled in the form below would like to be more careful, hard working, thoughtful, and polite, and a bit more affectionate. Different pairs of adjectives, describing other facets of personality, character, and behaviour, could yield results

A completed self-perception form

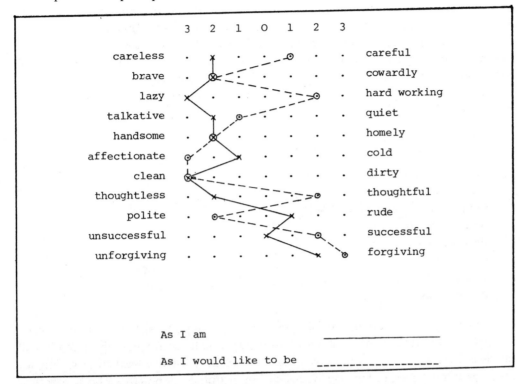

leading to the perception of different targets for personal change. As with check lists, the relevance of this exercise can be increased substantially by asking the people with the problems to generate their own lists of adjectives for inclusion on the scales.

Self-perception forms can also be used in other ways. Individuals may rate themselves 'as others see me' and then compare their results with those obtained when they are rated by others, either individually or in groups. This could be treated as a measure of the 'insight' possessed by people about the way they are perceived by other people, but care should be taken not to read too much into a single, simple pencil-and-paper exercise. Its results should never be seen as significant on their own.

INTERVIEWS

The interview is the universal tool of the helper; it can be used almost anytime, by anyone, for almost any purpose. Introducing it at this point is not meant to imply that it should be restricted to assessing 'self', but some of its uses can be illustrated as well here as anywhere else.

In tune with the rest of the approach, interviews should not be seen as the exclusive preserve of the professional, but rather as something which group members can practise with each other, with equally valuable results. At its most basic, the 'peer interview', as it is sometimes rather grandly called, can take the form of a 'buzz' exercise in which the group member turns to the person next to him and conducts an informal discussion on a given topic for a brief period. If 'self' is the subject, the interviews may be given a minimal structure by suggesting that each person finds out from his partner something about:

the best job I ever had
the worst job I ever had
my best points
my worst points
the person I would most like to be
why I am here today
things I like
things I hate
people I like
people I dislike.

After a specified period, anything from a couple of minutes to half an hour, each interviewer reports back his findings to the group, and these are then discussed. It will be clear that interviews conducted like this not only yield useful information for assessment purposes, but they also provide opportunities for practising both interview technique (making preparations, asking good questions, listening to answers, pursuing themes, responding to the mood of the interviewee, and summarizing results at the end) and, of course, the corresponding activities for the person being interviewed. Both are 'take-away' assets with applications in innumerable situations.

SEVEN-POINT PLAN

More structured versions of the interview can also be used in this way. Alec Rodger's 'seven-point plan' is a well-known assessment and interview format which can be given to group members to guide their interviews with each other. It was originally designed to assess candidates for jobs, but in this context it acts as a check list covering the following personal areas:

(1) *physical attributes* such as the individual's body build, basic physical proportions, level of fitness, and state of health; and the state of his or her eyesight or hearing;

(2) *attainments* of the individual, including educational and professional qualifica-

tions, work record, and so on, but also including other areas such as sport, games, and talents of any kind;

(3) *general ability* as ascertained by cognitive tests (e.g. I.Q.), and ability to use words, numbers, and spatial thinking;

(4) *special aptitudes* of any kind: the list of these is almost endless, but the most important might include scientific or mechanical ability, literary or artistic aptitudes, manual skills of many kinds, memory, and working with people;

(5) *interests*, which are, of course, often the key to an individual's life, much more than anything else about him; we are interested here in both the kinds of thing he may be interested in, and the range of his interests;

(6) *personality factors*, which more than anything else distinguish one individual from another: what is this person like? We can use a great many concepts to think about this, including introversion/extraversion, dependency, anxiety, friendliness, sense of humour, attitudes to authority, confidence and self-esteem, dominance, and so on. Often, however, an understanding of an individual will only come from finding out how he sees things for himself;

(7) *circumstances*, which refer to the particulars of the way an individual is living at the time and how these affect what he wants to do. Under this heading would be family circumstances, accommodation, financial circumstances, plus any problems that may be current at the time.

Working through these points in an interview and making notes about them will help groups or individuals start to get an organized overall picture of themselves. They could also use it to spot gaps where they think they need to find out more about themselves.

Knowing

Assessing someone's stock of knowledge is a relatively straightforward matter, as long as any suggestion of an 'examination' is avoided. Literate individuals will sometimes be willing to write what amounts to an essay about a personal problem but most people prefer to avoid anything that reminds them, however distantly, of their schooldays. More informal methods can however achieve the same results. Simply asking someone, in an unstructured interview, what he knows about the subject under consideration (the Housing Department's points system, the Judges' Rules, or the effects of over-eating on the body) is one way of starting. So is a group discussion, although it is unlikely to identify very exactly any areas of ignorance. It can, however, extend awareness of what needs to be known, how information has helped others to solve problems, where it can be obtained, and who in the group holds information of potential use to someone else.

A more precise assessment is possible with sentence completion, e.g.

The best places to look for jobs are ....

The place to complain about a solicitor is ....

You can get housing advice at the ....

But the most accurate plotting of information deficits is obtainable with multiple choice questions:

The legal limit for alcohol in a driver's bloodstream is:

☐ 10 milligrams per 100 millilitres
☐ 64 milligrams per 100 millilitres
☐ 80 milligrams per 100 millilitres
☐ 120 milligrams per 100 millilitres.

Tick the correct answer.

Questions like these can quite easily be assembled for any area of information which is being assessed. High scores will suggest that whatever else the cause of the problem may be, it is not want of information. Low scores will pinpoint deficits of a very specific kind, which need to be put right at a later stage of the process.

Feeling

Feelings are sometimes assumed to be buried deep in the recesses of the human mind, accessible only to skilled probing by sophisticated methods. But the feelings that cause problems for individuals are most often those that surface too frequently or too transparently, making existing situations worse, or creating fresh difficulties where none existed previously. The feelings may be anything from mild anger to deep and disabling depression, and their effects can range from a modest impairment of family relationships to the most extreme violence.

It is with these manifest feelings that problem solving concerns itself in the first place, and there is no shortage of techniques for evoking and dealing quite directly with some of them.

Sentence completion is, as usual, a source of inspiration:

I feel sad when ....

When I am late for work I feel ....

It's all right for people who ....

Traffic Wardens are ....

And pattern notes will help portray the comet's tail of feeling that most major problems trail behind them. Possible titles for pattern notes on feelings might be:

sex, violence, anger, fear, bosses, women, men, work, marriage, children, honesty, officials, us and them.

Points that emerge from either sentence completion or pattern notes can be further explored in interviews conducted by staff members or other participants. Interviews are probably the most frequently used method for examining personal feelings, and not much need be said about them here, except to emphasize that, in a problem-solving context, any records of the encounter should be surrendered to the interviewee for his safekeeping.

The most prolific of the available techniques for measuring feelings and attitudes are those of questionnaires and personality inventories, of which there are literally hundreds to choose from. A great many of them are standardized tests which must be administered by a qualified tester, usually a psychologist. If you want to use this sort of measure you should secure the services of a psychologist who is sympathetic to what you are doing and who is prepared to read back results to the individuals who have completed tests, and to give them the fullest possible interpretation of their likely significance.

Otherwise there are numerous non-protected tests which can be obtained and used; Eysenck's *Know Your Own Personality*, for example, contains scales which deal with assertiveness, aggression, sexual attitudes, and masculinity and femininity. Nor is it too difficult to compose simple scales of your own to help group members express their feelings about something, e.g.

I feel anxious . . .

never   sometimes   frequently   all the time.

Underline the word that applies to you.

PICTURES

Questionnaires should not, however, be over-used, and one way of avoiding the tedium of too much writing is to use pictures to stimulate thought and discussion during the assessment period. Some people seem to respond more readily to photographs or cartoons of human situations than to written or spoken descriptions. These need not be specially produced for assessment purposes: we are surrounded by suitable materials in books, newspapers, and magazines. Below is an example of the kind of picture that can be cut out of a magazine and mounted on a piece of paper with a question typed beneath it to provoke discussion. In this case the aim is to look at how people make judgements concerning the emotional states of others, and to raise some questions concerning relations between the sexes.

Pictures like this will not produce precise results, but if they are appropriate to the problem being looked at, they will help to disclose aspects of attitudes and experience not tapped by more formal methods.

Jealousy

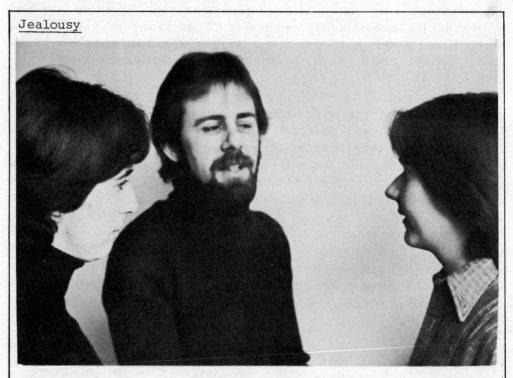

One of the people in this picture is jealous of another one. Which one is it? and why?

The temptation should, however, be resisted to use pictures of this sort as an amateur 'projective test' in which the innermost ideas and intimate fantasies of the 'subject' are spilled out in a flood, sometimes to the discomfort and embarrassment of the person concerned. Pictures, tests, and interviews should all be treated as the prelude to group discussion about the issues they have raised in the minds of those involved. Group discussion is a particularly suitable forum for the expression and exploration of feelings. But this need not be done in an incoherent, 'feeling' way. Instead, the topic for discussion should be announced, e.g. 'disappointments in life', and it should then be pursued in a purposeful, rational, and acceptable way. It is no part of the approach presented in this book to provoke people into displays of emotion they might later regret. And there is no place in it for the calculated use of 'silence', or for slightly coercive interpretation by the 'leader', or the simulation of 'therapeutic' anger.

Doing

'Doing' really comprises two separate but related aspects of behaviour: the manner in which people actually tackle some of their problems; and their past experience, which will typically contain a mixture of strengths and weaknesses. The best way of assessing the first of these aspects – the skill with which individuals conduct themselves in social situations – is to observe them as they happen.

OBSERVATION

Observation as an assessment technique concerns itself with three things:

1 capturing the 'bits' of behaviour to be observed;
2 methods for analysing and making sense of them; and
3 developing observation skills.

The best kind of behaviour to observe is that which occurs in real life. This is sometimes relatively easy to arrange. Drinking behaviour in pubs, for example, being assertive in queues, or striking up a conversation with a stranger can be observed and reported on by a fellow group member, or by someone else.

There are other kinds of behaviour which are not so easily observed in this way, either because the situations are spontaneous ones such as a row with a family member, or because an observer would be seen as an intruder – in a job interview, for instance. These and many other bits of behaviour may need therefore to be simulated in some way. The most direct way of doing this is to stage a role-play in which a situation is described, a set of characters invented, and the whole of the incident re-enacted as though it were in real life. Here is an example of a structured role-play dealing with a common problem at work:

Conflict at work: late again

JOE is late for work for the fourth day running at the factory where he works. He is anxious not to lose the job because he has two young children, a lot of H.P. commitments, and he drinks quite a lot.

ALF is the foreman of the shop where Joe works. He has a big contract job to complete and if one worker is late, it slows down the whole line. He finds Joe a good worker but feels that he must do something about his repeated lateness.

TED is the shop steward and he has come along with Joe to the interview with Alf, to keep an eye on things and to protect the interests of his union colleague.

These parts are assigned to three people who then play out the interview that ensues, for about five or ten minutes. The rest of the group observe the role-play and comment on how effectively each played his part and what would actually have happened.

There are a great many ready-made role-plays in existence covering a wide range of subjects but, as the example above shows, it is not difficult to construct new ones for use with a particular problem. Role-plays can vary in their complexity and in their degree of specificity. Some are highly structured and come complete with a script whereas others provide just an outline of the situation, so that participants can invest their own feelings and perceptions in the performance. How much structure is used will depend to a large extent upon the make-up of particular groups and how much knowledge of the problem is held by the group.

Some people are naturally adept at role-play and enjoy it endlessly. Others refuse point-blank to take part at all. But, providing the situations are realistic and within the experience of the participants, most people soon get over their initial reluctance, especially after seeing one or two performances by those more confident than themselves.

Simulations, which are more structured variants of role-play, can also be used for assessing behaviour but, since they embody a large learning element, they will be dealt with in the learning chapter.

Another form of behaviour which lends itself to observation is that which occurs in groups. This can be made more visible by adopting a 'goldfish-bowl' format, in which some members of a larger group conduct their discussion in the centre of the room, whilst their colleagues look on. Although it is more limited in range than role-play, there is a lot to be learned from observing someone at work in a group and feeding back comments to him afterwards.

With both role-play and group behaviour, there are three main ways in which observations can be made. The first of them is for observers to watch the proceedings and to report their findings to the participants in a fairly impressionistic form. This has the advantage of not requiring any prior preparation, but it may lack precision, and it leaves no permanent record for subsequent use in the problem-solving process.

A second and more vivid way of recording relevant activities is to use an audio- or video-tape machine. These are fairly widely available and can often be borrowed from educational or training establishments. Its great advantage is that it enables the 'actors' to see an action-replay of their performances and to evaluate them in a way that is not possible during a single 'live' presentation. The recordings can also be reviewed on subsequent occasions and used to gauge progress in changing behaviour in desired directions. Video has another virtue, that of privacy; an individual can view his own behaviour by himself and draw his own conclusions from what he sees.

Third, whether the behaviour is recorded in this way or not, the quality and sharpness of the observations can be improved substantially by using simple pencil-and-paper measures as well.

The most basic record of behaviour is a straight count of the number of times a given event occurs during a given time. Examples might be the number of contributions made to a conversation by an individual, or by each of several parties involved. A speech might be monitored for the number of times the speaker says 'um' or 'er', the number of smiles, the number of gestures, or the number of encouraging or positive points made. The choice depends entirely on the purpose of the exercise; but it is unlikely that only one category of behaviour would be used. A number of categories can be recorded for several participants by constructing a schedule like this one:

Observing group behaviour: recording schedule

Behaviour type	Number of contributions made by participants							
	Tom	Bill	Jean	Mary				
Information seeking								
Information giving								
Supportive comments								
Aggressive comments								
Total contributions								

Alternatively, a rating scale can be used, rather than a simple check list. If the session has been recorded on video-tape, individuals can rate themselves as well, when the recording is replayed. If the session involves self-presentation in a talk or interview, individuals can rate themselves on the dimensions shown in *Putting Myself Across*, below. This is a check list, but rating scales could easily be added using, for example, a five-point scale.

PUTTING MYSELF ACROSS

Giving a talk about myself

When you watch and listen to yourself on video, try to think of how well you are doing certain things. Draw a circle around the word at the right-hand side of the page that describes your reaction.

Name _____

1.	I heard every word that was said	Yes	No
2.	I used a forceful opening	Yes	No
3.	I looked straight at the audience	Yes	No
4.	I used an appropriate body posture	Yes	No
5.	I talked to the audience	Yes	No
6.	I kept people's attention throughout	Yes	No
7.	I looked somewhat uneasy	Yes	No
8.	I seemed confident	Yes	No
9.	I managed to say what I wanted to say	Yes	No
10.	I ended on a positive note	Yes	No

Think of how you acted in general. What kinds of change do you think you would have to make for some of the following situations? How well do you think you would handle them?

- an interview for a job
- an interview with a landlady about accommodation
- trying to cool down an argument
- being interviewed at the DHSS
- making a complaint in a shop
- being stopped by a policeman in the street.

Adapted from Saskatchewan Newstart (1977) *Lifeskills Coaching Manual* (Prince Albert, Saskatchewan: Department of Manpower and Immigration).

It makes even more sense if the participants in such an exercise generate their own scoring categories before completing the task to be observed, using brainstorming, pattern notes, or a group discussion for the purpose.

In other situations, too, the problem solver must sometimes stand witness to his own behaviour, past and present, and there are pencil-and-paper methods to help him testify to its nature and effectiveness. This might consist of a 'home-made' social skills check list looking at some of the things that go on in face-to-face interaction, and at some of the larger problems people face in their daily lives.

A social skills check list

Interacting with others	I do this well		
	Always	Sometimes	Never
1 Looking someone in the eyes			
2 Entering a room full of people			
3 Responding reasonably to personal criticism			
Handling problems			
1 Making decisions and sticking to them			
2 Planning my leisure time			
3 Resisting pressure to do something I don't want to do			

The list of possible items for inclusion in this sort of check list is endless, limited only by the needs of the people with whom you are working and your own imagination. The answers can be made more precise by adding a rating scale, e.g.

I can tell jokes:

Very well └────────────┴────────────┴────────────┴────────────┘ Not at all well

A slightly less structured way of finding out how someone behaves in certain circumstances is to use sentence completion, as with the touchy young man overleaf.

EXPERIENCE

'Experience' is not so much concerned with *how* people do things as with *what* they have done or are currently doing. Its importance from an assessment point of view lies

I LOSE MY TEMPER WHEN...

1 I Tell Pepol to Lay off me
   + they will not.

2 When Pepol keep pushing me
   around...

3 When I am out with a bird
   + they No I have been going
   stedy with her for some
   time + they call her a
   pro or slag.

4 when I am told to get out
   of a pub when I have done
   nothing rong to enybody +
   that person is not the gaffer.

in the possibility that a survey of experience may reveal unexpected patterns in people's lives, identify strengths as well as weaknesses, and draw attention to changes which could be made to help them cope better with some personal problem.

Such a large subject can obviously be approached from many directions, none of them necessarily superior to any other. One person may feel most comfortable just thinking, and possibly making some notes about features of his experience. Another may prefer to talk to someone else, either informally or in a more structured interview designed to elicit information about some specific aspect of his past. Group discussion, too, will often revolve around the concrete experience of its members – sometimes funny, sometimes sad, almost always interesting, and, in the average group, amazingly diverse. Ways of stimulating and sustaining activities along these lines should occur readily by now to most readers, but there are numerous exercises which can be used for the purpose.

If someone is looking for recurring difficulties in his past experience, one way of helping him to do so is to provide a 'history form' on which events and situations can be entered in a roughly chronological order, as on this accommodation history form.

Accommodation history form

Address	Type of accommodation	Dates occupied	Rent	Drawbacks	Reason for leaving

Depending on the nature of the programme and the problems of the participants, more or less detail can be recorded using this basic form. For example, details such as number of rooms, number of occupants, facilities shared with other tenants, structural repairs needed, how the accommodation was found, relations with landlord, relations with other tenants, and many others could be added.

Past experience is not, however, just a record of neutral events, or of things that have gone wrong; it should also be treated as a repository of growth points around which successful problem-solving strategies can be constructed. A format for doing this in relation to previous employment is provided by surveying marketable skills.

SURVEYING MARKETABLE SKILLS

This exercise has been freely adapted from the Saskatchewan Newstart *Life Skills Coaching Manual* (1973) and is intended to help individuals with superficially poor work experience to spot possible assets which they could offer to a prospective employer. It is useful to start by taking a job held by many men with histories of casual and seasonal employment, that of a barman, and subjecting its performance to a simple skills analysis. The qualities required may be 'brainstormed' and most groups will come up with twenty or so items. These can be divided in various ways, including the one shown on the form below, distinguishing 'job skills' (which are specific to particular occupations) from 'hidden skills' (which have applications across a range of jobs). With this example in mind the rest of the form is filled in by listing, not necessarily in their correct order, all or some of the jobs previously held by the participant. There are jobs

---

Surveying marketable skills

On this sheet list the jobs you have done in the first column, the job skills which you have performed well in the second column, and any 'hidden skills' you feel relevant to the job in the third column.

Jobs I have had	Job skills I performed well	Hidden skills I performed well
Example: Barman	1) Pouring drinks correctly 2) Cellar work 3) Mixing drinks 4) Charging correct amount 5) Working the till 6) Giving efficient service 7) Keeping bar stocked up	1) Sociable 2) Good memory (stock layout, prices, etc.) 3) Good at mental arithmetic 4) Good timekeeper 5) Got on with workmates

which almost defy the optimistic tone of the exercise, e.g. packer, or general warehouseman; but the time spent on it, which can be as long as two hours in all, will usually be repaid with a list of skills and personal qualities. They can then be combined and recombined into possible jobs not previously thought to be within the competence of the person concerned.

TIME

Experience is not always filled with activity as socially approved as work, and the passage of time, whether it is well spent or misspent, is often seen as a burden by the poor, the unemployed, or the emotionally impoverished. It is worth looking at time, therefore, in quite an organized fashion.

Diary forms
Small units of time can be examined with the aid of a diary form which makes it possible, over a given period, to scrutinize the timing of critical events or incidents. A typical form divides each day into a number of sections, and provides space for several days to be inserted.

Diary form

Day	Morning	Afternoon	Evening

The best way to fill in a diary form is daily, as events happen; but if it is used in retrospect it will help to reconstruct what happened in the period immediately prior to some personal crisis, such as being dismissed from a job, or breaking up a relationship, or being admitted to an institution. If the *Day* column on the form is left blank, it may be filled in from any one day to another, for example, from seven days before a critical incident. When groups of people fill in diary forms it can also be useful to look at common patterns of time use and abuse.

Diary forms can also be adapted to look at particular pieces of behaviour, drinking, for example – when it happens, who with, where, the cost, and so forth.

Snakes

Larger tracts of time are better handled by what some people call 'lifelines' but which we have renamed 'snakes' for reasons that will become obvious in the next chapter. It consists of a line drawn on a sheet of paper to represent the course of someone's life, or some part of it in which they are particularly interested. On this line are inscribed significant life events, with approximate indications of time, some description of what happened, and a commentary on the feelings that accompanied the action.

A completed 'snake' like the one on page 49 can open up new perspectives in the individual's view of his past, illuminating particular events and periods and suggesting hitherto 'invisible' patterns of behaviour and attitudes. But like all assessment methods it will not work for all of the people all of the time, and alternatives may have to be used.

Using assessment methods

This brief review of assessment has followed the contours of the problem-solving process itself: defining the problem, exploring it in more detail, taking it apart, and inspecting the pieces. In doing so it has introduced and described a variety of techniques drawn from many sources. They can be broadly summarized under four main headings:

1 pencil and paper
2 interviews
3 group discussion and
4 observation.

Each has a distinctive contribution to make to the assessment stage of personal problem solving, but because of their relative under-use, and the ease with which they can be presented in a printed medium, pencil-and-paper methods have absorbed a disproportionate amount of the space in this chapter. This is the reverse of what happens in practice, and in the notes which follow some suggestions are made about ways in which different types of assessment can be used to the best advantage of individuals and groups in search of answers to their problems.

PENCIL-AND-PAPER METHODS

Of all the assessment methods, those that involve the use of pencil and paper are the most neglected by the helping agencies. Among the reasons for this may be the feeling that they are either inappropriate or are too difficult to administer. Another reason is that people on the receiving end tend to associate tests with exams and schooling, and the sinister mysteries of psychological testing.

These understandable resistances can be countered in a number of ways. First,

Snakes

Imagine that the 'snake' below represents your life. Starting from
your childhood, can you think of the events, people, or places that
were turning points for you. Mark these on the 'snake' starting at
the top. Also mark in things that were important to you at different
times, and show how these led to where you are now.

AGE

(5) Serious accident at school - teachers very kind.

(6) Get new bike for Christmas.

(9) Join Cubs - get a new uniform and lots of badges.

(11) Fear of 11 plus - didn't finish it and sent to Sec. Mod. school.

(12) Broke my leg at Scout Camp. Off school for several weeks.

(13) Promoted to Patrol Leader in Scouts.

(14) Got my 1st Class badge in Scouts. Started going steady with girlfriend. Stopped going to Scouts.

(15) First real drink - vodka - drank ½ bottle and passed out.

(16) Left school - got job in exciting world of horse racing.

(19) Joined Army as driver. Met wife.

(20) Got married - 1st child. Got drunk for 3 days. Emotional problems - drinking a lot - ½ bottle whisky a day.

(22) Court-martial - kicked out of Army because of being drunk in charge of Scout car.

(23) Wife left me - was drinking all the time.

Present - in hospital 'drying out'.

You can use more sheets and draw 'snakes' of your own, if you wish...

many of the exercises described in this chapter do not conform to what most people think of as a test, and most of them do not demand a high level of reading and writing skills. Second, the purpose of all the activities is carefully and clearly explained in advance so that no-one is asked to complete a form 'blindfold'. Third, when completed most of the exercises yield results that are either self-evident or capable of immediate self-scoring. Where this is not possible, as with some of the more formal tests, then the scores or results are read back at the earliest opportunity. Finally, the filling in of forms and tests should be seen as a learnable skill of some value in its own right in a modern, bureaucratic society.

The problem of widespread aversion to the idea of filling in forms and tests can be overcome to some extent by providing an introduction, which might consist of very simple and possibly slightly frivolous examples of the major types likely to be encountered during the remainder of the programme. The first piece of paper to go in a participant's file, for example, could be a basic self-description form of the kind that is often used in job applications. Individuals who do this badly may like to practice filling in other forms in common use, applying for a driving licence, or to join a club. And another kind of questionnaire item – the check list – can be introduced in the following way:

Which of the following forms have you ever filled in?

☐ Driving licence application   ☐ Club membership
☐ Insurance proposal   ☐ Football pools
☐ Job application   ☐ Hire-purchase agreement

Tick the ones that apply to you.

A preliminary session on forms and tests will also identify individuals with poor reading and writing skills. The totally illiterate can still participate in pencil-and-paper assessment by dictating their responses to someone else, usually a staff member, and there need be no undue delay in the proceedings. But, even in a normally literate group, the length of time it takes the members to fill in particular pieces of paper will vary widely, and this does pose problems of pace, timing, and boredom for the person running the session. Where groups contain some very slow and some very fast writers, a balance has to be struck between allowing some of them to become bored and making sure that the rest have had time to record most of what they want to say. Experience will provide rough guides to how long is needed to complete specific pieces of pencil-and-paper work.

We have also found that filling in forms and tests can sometimes act as a stimulus for people with literacy problems to seek out remedial education in reading and writing so that they can keep up with the others.

A final word of caution about pencil-and-paper assessment methods: the profusion of available questionnaires and the ease with which you can construct your own are an ever-present invitation to over-use. This should be resisted at all costs. Most people have a tolerance to filling in forms, which is strictly limited. This varies from individual to individual and from group to group. In practice over-use will quickly provoke signals of anguish and boredom, which should be heeded; but a simple rule of thumb is that not more than 10 per cent of the total time available in a programme should be spent wielding the pencil.

INTERVIEWS

Interviews need little explanation: they are really extensions of everyday conversation. They are also perhaps the most widely used helping method in counselling, social work, and vocational guidance. The fact that a relatively small part of this book is devoted to interviewing is not intended to devalue its importance in the problem-solving process. Many of the methods already described, and some of those in later chapters, are effective because they provoke in the people who take part in them a variety of thoughts and feelings. Sometimes these remain, essentially, private reactions, but often the participant will want to discuss what he is finding out, either within the group or, more personally, with someone else.

Interviews should therefore be built into the assessment programme in two ways. They should form part of the general exploration of problem areas, looking at past experience, at strengths and weaknesses, and at attitudes. But they should also be available on demand for any group member who feels it would be helpful at any point in his self-assessment. Within the framework of group problem solving this is easier to say than to do, since time is always the commodity in shortest supply. But the offer of personal interviews should always be made, and met, as often as is practicable. And as with every other activity, the results of any interview, if they are recorded in any way, should become the property of the person who has been interviewed.

Much unnecessary mystification surrounds many discussions of interviews and interviewing technique, but its uses in this approach are of a straightforward and common-sense nature. If an interview is defined as a conversation with a purpose, then just giving it a title such as 'family problems' or 'welfare rights' immediately imparts to it some degree of structure. However, a fact-finding or assessment interview is likely to be a bit more organized than that. The '5 W–H' formula described earlier is one way of structuring an interview without too much preparation. And Alec Rodger's 'Seven Points' have already been suggested as an example of a highly organized and pre-

prepared interview plan. Less detailed outlines for use in interviews are easily composed and, although they should not be adhered to too slavishly, they do provide a
series of pegs upon which to hang the points that emerge from a dialogue. An interview
about money problems might be structured like this:

Money in your life

1 Experience of money
- pocket money
- part time jobs whilst at school
- first job, first pay-packet
- current position, average
  income
- other sources of income

2 Expenditure
- essential expenditure
- savings
- debts
- leisure costs

3 Money problems
- budgeting ability
- unpaid debts, HP, overdrafts, etc.
- borrowing money
- reducing expenditure

4 Personal meanings of
money
- time spent thinking about money
- arguments about money
  matters
- coping with a pools win.

This list could be used to phrase questions in the order shown, dealing with one
point after the other, or the interviewee could be encouraged to talk about the problem
in a biographical way, the interviewer checking off points as they are covered. Any
remaining points could be picked up at the end.

Really skilled interviewers can sometimes work without any kind of preparation,
simply allowing the conversation to develop its own internal structure and letting the

information emerge in a natural way; but when time is in short supply some kind of plan is probably essential.

GROUP DISCUSSION

Even more is made of the difficulties of running group discussions than of conducting interviews. The use of discussion in groupwork and therapy has been written about extensively, but a lot of this work can safely be ignored since the use of group discussion for assessment purposes is quite different from group therapy.

During assessment, the main uses of group discussion include:

- opportunities to discuss the meaning and relevance of assessment
- exchanges of experience
- a chance to learn about other people
- expression of attitudes and opinions
- feedback on personal opinions and behaviour
- practice in presenting a point of view to a group of people.

These aims can be written on a wall chart and displayed so that participants can refer back to them at any time. The achievement of these aims does not require lengthy training or great expertise, just adequate preparation, courteous administration, and some practice.

The amount of preparation that is necessary to ensure a useful and effective discussion depends on many things: the timing of the discussion, the nature of the topic, the make-up of the group in terms of personality, attitudes, and problems, and the experience and interests of the group leader.

If the discussion follows some particularly stimulating activity, such as a pencil-and-paper exercise, or a series of peer interviews, then elaborate planning will not be needed to keep the discussion going or to generate useful information and ideas. If a discussion is to be started from scratch, however, some thought should be given to finding a lively stimulus to get things moving. This could be the presentation of a case history or the description of a situation by the group leader, a short talk by a guest speaker, or even by a member of the group on some particular topic, a film or tape-recording, or a cartoon.

Once discussion has started only a minimum of direction may be needed to keep it to the topic and to ensure that as many people as possible make their contributions. A list of headings similar to the interview 'prompts' can be prepared in advance and checked off by the group leader as they are covered. It is a good idea to finish the discussion whilst it is still in full swing rather than waiting for it to die, as long as everyone has had time to make his contribution and an individual is not cut off abruptly in mid-sentence, or before he has finished making his point. At the end, a brief summary can be made and put into context with the programme activities that have preceded and will follow the particular session. It may also be useful to record on a wall chart or blackboard the main points that were raised and agreed upon during the discussion.

Whenever the opportunity arises, large groups should be broken down into smaller ones, preferably on a self-selected membership basis, to consider and report back on some separate aspects of a larger topic. For example, if the main topic of discussion is leisure, small groups could be set up to consider the following aspects:

> - leisure activities that are free
> - sport
> - evening classes
> - hobbies
> - meeting people
> - pub games.

After ten or twenty minutes the small groups could be asked to report their findings back, each group selecting a spokesman.

The 'results' of group discussion, like those obtained in interviews, are different in kind from the output of forms and tests, more diffuse and less easily expressed in words or on wall sheets. But they are no less useful in allowing individuals to explore and do something practical about their personal problems.

The uses of assessment

In this chapter we have looked at some examples from a whole range of available assessment methods and techniques. The coverage is not exhaustive – in a book this size it could not be – nor have all the uses of each exercise been catalogued. But the chapter will have served its purpose if it has indicated the great wealth of material that is there for the taking, and for the making, since the essence of this approach in action is its flexibility and adaptability. Its success depends on the creativity with which workers weave some of these elements into attractive and effective assessment programmes for use with particular groups or individuals. They may appropriate or invent highly specific methods, or they may make use of some of the 'standard' methods, which can be turned in the direction of any subject under the sun. Some of these are summarized in this table, using the *knowing*, *feeling*, and *doing* classification. It should be emphasized that adopting these three categories does not mean trying to reduce every personal problem into *knowing*, *feeling*, and *doing* components in a mechanical and unthinking way. Many problems are composite in nature and will defy all attempts to pin neat labels on them.

Assessment: section of the curriculum matrix

	Knowing	*Feeling*	*Doing*
Assessment	Tests, essays, examinations, check lists, information-gathering interviews, situation tests	Questionnaires, rating scales, sentence completion, projective techniques, pattern notes, group discussion, counselling, self-report, introspection	Task performance and observation, skill analysis, life histories, role-play, fishbowl groups, 'objective' measures

Note: See page 139 for the completed curriculum matrix

Finally, assessment is not a once-and-for-all event, but a continuing process in a problem-solving cycle. Although it has been presented here as a separate phase of activity, it will be clear that many of the methods reach forward into later stages of problem solving, producing immediately obvious personal objectives, and contributing strongly to learning, as well as lending themselves to use as evaluation measures. Each of these stages in turn feeds back to the assessment stage to complete a loop which can be used within a single session or as the basis of a series of meetings.

It is also important to have realistic expectations of assessment. None of the methods described here will produce magical results. They are unlikely to reveal totally unsuspected aspects of personality, and they are equally unlikely to disclose astonishing hidden talents.

What they do offer is a common-sense and systematic framework for collecting a wide range of information which can then be used to pursue the solution to some personal problem. They also represent a tool-kit of methods which individuals can acquire and take away with them for future use.

The tangible results of the assessment stage will be a personal file containing all the pencil-and-paper exercises completed by the individual together with reports of interviews, group discussions, and observations made by others, plus copies of hand-outs which describe the methods and procedures. These results are never final; assessment is always something that is 'in progress'. But there comes a time when it is appropriate to draw a line beneath the data already assembled and to make a summary of it in readiness for the next stage of the process: setting personal objectives.

Notes and references

Assessment is so wide a subject and relevant materials are so profusely available that these references will scarcely begin to do them justice. And yet there is no single introduction to the field which can be recommended to anyone wishing to work in the way described in this book. There are technical accounts on test construction and validation designed for psychologists, and some parts of books devoted to larger issues such as groupwork or counselling contain useful items. Otherwise the methods and materials are scattered through the literature in journals, books, manuals, and training packages waiting to be garnered by the persistent and the inquisitive.

This brief guide to some starting points for the search is organized under three principal heads: those of interviewing, pencil-and-paper methods, and group discussion.

INTERVIEWS

Despite its central importance for social work and other helping functions, interviewing somehow defies encapsulation in books and articles. There is the classic brief account by E. and K. de Schweinitz (1962) *Interviewing in the Social Services; an Introduction* (London: NCSS), and many others attempt to define and improve the skills of the interviewer. See, for example: W. V. Bingham, B. V. Moore, and J. W. Gustad (1959) *How to Interview* (New York: Harper and Row); E. Sidney and M. Brown (1961) *The Skills of Interviewing* (London: Tavistock); A. Garrett (1948) *Interviewing: Its Principles and Merits* (New York: Family Services Association of America); and C. P. Cross (1974) *Interviewing and Communication in Social Work* (London: Routledge and Kegan Paul). However, for a cautionary view of the merits of interviewing as an assessment tool, read the chapter on Assessment of Men in H. J. Eysenck (1953) *Uses and Abuses of Psychology* (Harmondsworth: Penguin). For a practical guide to the business of being an interviewee, see T. M. Higham (1971) *Your First Interview* (London: Cornmarket). And for the method referred to on page 34 see A. Rodger (1974) *Seven Point Plan* (Windsor: N.F.E.R.).

PENCIL-AND-PAPER METHODS

Questionnaires and tests are traditionally the preserve of the professional psychologist, and most of the published work in this area addresses itself to him or his customers: psychiatrists, employers, teachers, etc. This is exemplified in R. B. Cattell (1965) *The Scientific Analysis of Personality* (Harmondsworth: Penguin). For a brief review of some formal testing methods, see F. N. Kerlinger (1964) *Foundations of Behavioural Research* (New York: Holt, Rhinehart and Winston). A fuller catalogue is contained in L. J. Cronbach (1970) *Essentials of Psychological Testing* (New York: Harper and Row).

If you want to avoid some of the common pitfalls in compiling tests and questionnaires it would be as well to consult a work like A. N. Oppenheim (1968) *Questionnaire Design and Attitude Measurement* (London: Heinemann), or J. Tiffin and E. J. McCormick (1966) *Industrial Psychology* (London: George Allen and Unwin). Two books by P. Vernon cover the whole business of testing intelligence and personality: (1969) *Personality Assessment: A Critical Survey* (London: Tavistock); and (1971) *Intelligence and Attainment Tests* (London: University of London Press).

A useful source of assessment material addressed to a wide range of concrete problems is Saskatchewan Newstart (1973) *Life Skills Coaching Manual* (Prince Albert, Saskatchewan: Department of Manpower and Immigration). The Mooney Problem Checklist is described in more detail in A. Anastasi (1976) *Psychological Testing* (4th edition; London: Collier-Macmillan).

There is a growing library of self-development manuals which combine the older tradition of self-improvement, e.g. D. Carnegie (1936) *How to Win Friends and Influence People* (New York: Simon and Schuster) and Pelmanism, with the insights of cognitive psychology. Many of them provide general assessment techniques, for instance, L. Sperry, D. J. Mickelson, and P. L. Hunsacker (1977) *You Can Make It Happen* (*A Guide to Self-Actualization and Organizational Change*) (Reading, Massachusetts: Addison-Wesley), or R. Sharpe and D. Lewis (1977) *The Success Factor* (London: Pan).

Transactional analysis, too, has developed a great many ways of helping people look at themselves, although these would normally form part of a coherent TA experience. See, for example, D. Jongeward and M. James (1973) *Winning with People: Group Exercises in Transactional Analysis* (London: Addison-Wesley).

Some specific techniques

Pattern notes, which have tremendous potential in social work, are the invention of T. Buzan; see (1974) *Use Your Head* (London: BBC Publications). This book also contains methods for improving reading, memory, and study techniques.

The most readily accessible formal tests are those in H. J. Eysenck (1962) *Know Your Own I.Q.* and (1966) *Check Your Own I.Q.* (Harmondsworth: Penguin), and H. J. Eysenck and G. Wilson (1976) *Know Your Own Personality* (Harmondsworth: Penguin). The first two books deal with self-administering I.Q. tests: general ones, and specific tests of verbal, numerical, and visuo-spatial abilities. *Know Your Own Personality* contains self-administering measures on extraversion-introversion, emotional stability, humour, sex, and social and political attitudes. The results should not be taken too seriously in isolation from other sorts of evidence but a lot of people seem to enjoy doing them, and the I.Q. scoring is probably on the generous side.

The main suppliers of tests in this country are N.F.E.R. Publishing Company Ltd., 2 Jennings Buildings, Thames Avenue, Windsor, Berks. SL4 1QS, and Hodder and Stoughton Ltd., P.O. Box 702, Mill Road, Dunton Green, Sevenoaks, Kent TN13 2YA.

Formal tests are often restricted to use by qualified psychologists or testers, but it is not usually difficult to find someone sympathetic to help in this way. There are a variety of assessment ideas in J. and M. Korving and M. Keeley (1975) *Out of the Rut* (London: BBC Publications) – a book for people looking for work.

For a detailed social skills check list see A. P. Goldstein, R. P. Sprafkin, and N. J. Gershaw (1976) *Skill Training for Community Living* (Oxford: Pergamon). This particular test was devised for use with psychiatric populations but can serve as a model for constructing your own check list for use with different groups. R. W. Novaco (1975) *Anger Control* (Lexington, Massachusetts: Lexington Books) describes an anger inventory. And for couples who want to explore their relationships, there is B. and C. Hopson (1973) *Twosome Plus: A Guide to Cohabitation with Exercises* (London: Bond and Briggs). See also E. Heimler (1975) *Survival in Society* (London: Weidenfeld and Nicolson). Heimler had developed and tested widely a 'scale of social functioning', which is referred to but not reproduced in this book. N. J. Bull (1969) *Moral Judgement from Childhood to Adolescence* (London: Routledge and Kegan Paul) describes some methods used in a research project on the development of moral judgement in schoolchildren; many of them are capable of adaptation to older age-groups.

These references are far from complete, but they do suggest some points of entry into a vast field; finding your own material is much more exciting and interesting. Most of it has to be adapted, in any case, to make it relevant and acceptable to the groups or individuals with whom you are working.

GROUP DISCUSSION

Group discussion and groupwork is another area which merits a book-length bibliography of its own. The best general introduction to the whole field is T. Douglas (1976) *Groupwork Practice* (London: Tavistock). But for the account of learning groups that is closest to the way they are used in social skills and personal problem solving, see M. L. J. Abercrombie (1970) *Aims and Techniques of Group Teaching* (London: Society for Research into Higher Education) and, also, the same author's earlier book (1969) *The Anatomy of Judgement* (Harmondsworth: Penguin).

Probably the best academic review of groups is D. Cartwright and A. Zander (eds.) (1968) *Group Dynamics* (London: Tavistock). And groups in a context of social skills are discussed in M. Argyle (1967) *The Psychology of Interpersonal Behaviour* (Harmondsworth: Penguin) and (1973) *Social Interaction* (London: Tavistock).

The work of R. F. Bales is of considerable importance and interest, particularly for anyone who is interested in using or developing ways of recording and making sense of the interaction in groups, e.g. R. F. Bales (1950) *Interaction Process Analysis: A Method for the Study of Small Groups* (Reading, Massachusetts: Addison-Wesley); and A. P. Hare, E. F. Borgatta, and R. F. Bales (1966) *Small Groups: Studies in Social Interaction* (New

York: Alfred Knopf). See also the chapter by R. F. Bales and F. L. Strodtbeck on Phases in Group Problem Solving in Cartwright and Zander (eds.) (1968).

There are also a great many descriptive and prescriptive accounts of groupwork, of which the following titles are typical examples: J. Klein (1966) *Working with Groups* (London: Hutchinson), which has useful chapters on role-play and group self-evaluation; E. Sidney, M. Brown, and M. Argyle (1973) *Skills with People* (London: Hutchinson), which is intended for managers in industry, but is good on group leading; and L. Button (1974) *Developmental Groupwork with Adolescents* (London: University of London Press).

The use of role-play in groups is touched upon in many groupwork texts; it is dealt with more fully in M. B. Miles (1971) *Learning to Work in Groups* (New York: Teachers College Press, Columbia University). The origins of role-play in psychodrama, and some of its current uses, are related in I. A. Greenberg (1974) *Psychodrama: Theory and Therapy* (London: Souvenir Press) – a book of readings, in which the authors include Moreno himself and Yablonsky. And, finally, two books which contain many exercises for use in group situations are: D. A. Kolb, I. M. Rubin, and J. McIntyre (1974) *Organizational Psychology: An Experiential Approach* (Englewood Cliffs, New Jersey: Prentice-Hall) (see particularly the Learning Styles Inventory on page 23); and D. W. Johnson and F. P. Johnson (1975) *Joining Together: Group Theory and Group Skills* (Englewood Cliffs, New Jersey: Prentice-Hall).

4 Setting objectives

The assessment stage, if it has worked properly, will have generated, for individuals and groups using this approach, a very large quantity of information: about themselves and their problems; about attitudes and feelings, strengths and weaknesses; and about areas in which it is obvious yet more information needs to be acquired. Should this be the case, the objectives which individuals will wish to set themselves become immediately obvious; they emerge without difficulty during assessment itself, clearly calling out for attention, and requiring little elaboration or clarification. This is what happens with a large number of problems: they may derive, in fact, from denials of the obvious, or evasion of unruly issues from sheer lack of confidence of being able to cope. Objective setting in these circumstances will be almost automatic: no sooner is a problem explored than it becomes apparent what needs to be done, and individuals can move on to the learning stage.

In other circumstances, however, people may need some help to crystallize their objectives into a form about which appropriate action can be taken, and in which the likelihood of its being taken will be increased. In addition it is sometimes necessary to divide objectives up in some way, according to how general or specific they are, or in terms of the time allotted to achieving them. A large, overall objective, for example, might only be tackled in a series of intermediate steps.

Chapter aims

The aims of this chapter, therefore, are to:

1 outline some characteristics of personal objectives which may help to get them clearer;

2 survey some methods of generating and setting personal objectives;

3 outline a straightforward process for use in setting objectives.

Before embarking on these, however, it may be helpful to discuss, briefly, the reasons for setting objectives.

During assessment, a number of thoughts on individuals' problems will have been generated; destinations will have become clearer, and levels of motivation given an initial test. A knowledge of how to set about coping with his problems is vital to a person's confidence and progress during the learning stage. In addition, some problems are complex and must be broken down into manageable stages leading towards possible solutions. Some of these stages will be attainable during the problem-solving session or course; others only after the course has been completed; and others still only after months or years, involving very long-term (and very thorough) planning. The setting of personal objectives will, however, give a pattern and purpose to the learning stage, and a chance for the individual to monitor his progress during it – and perhaps achieve some of his objectives. He can, in any case, take away with him at the end of the session or course a record of what he wishes to achieve and how he might set about achieving it – tied to some suitable time scale which he has decided for himself.

Characteristics of personal objectives

In its simplest and most useful form, a personal objective is a highly specific, clear statement of intention, regarding something that an individual is to achieve, or a general goal possibly to be reached by a number of subsidiary steps. Here are some examples:

By the end of this week I want to have painted the front door.

Tonight I will go to the pub at 9 p.m. rather than 8 p.m.

I am looking for a job as a fitter.

I want to save £40 to buy a new suit of clothes.

I would like to find out my right of access to my children.

I need to find out more about legal aid.

Next time I meet . . . I must be more pleasant to him.

I'm going to cut down smoking from sixty to forty cigarettes a day.

We're going to get married in a year's time.

People, of course, make many statements of this kind every day. When in the midst of problems, however, their ability to think clearly and arrive at decisions – even about simple courses of action – quickly diminishes. To arrive at the most useful kinds of personal objectives, we need to answer some basic questions in turn, for example:

- What exact course of action is involved? What will be done?
- When should it be done by?
- Where will it be done?
- Who will do it? Will it be done alone or in a group?
- What help or resources will be needed?
- How will I decide whether it has worked or not?
- Why this objective and not others? Can it for example be broken down into more easily managed parts?

It would be possible to construct a chart of these questions, and only to decide on a particular objective after choosing one for which all the above questions could be answered. This could, on the other hand, produce an inflexibility which might hamper individuals' progress; the above are really ideal situations to aim for and key questions to ask. They may furnish a direction in which to go; but many objectives can hardly be expected to conform to them in every detail.

Personal objectives then are, ideally:

- written down
- specific
- clear
- tied to a stated time period: short, long-term, or permanent
- provisional.

The last characteristic of objectives mentioned here reflects the fact that, as learning progresses, some objectives may change: some may broaden in scope and some become narrower; others may be considerably modified or transformed completely. It is best if objectives have a built-in flexibility, or provisional status, to allow desirable changes to be incorporated.

In addition, the question arises as to whether the objectives should or should not be public. It is likely that if people make their objectives public they will be more inclined to go some way towards achieving them. However, this should be up to the individual concerned: he may or may not wish to share his objectives with others, or he may wish to make some public and not others.

Methods for generating objectives

PROFILES OF PROBLEM AREAS

This is a pencil-and-paper method that leans very heavily on the material drawn out of assessment. For any individual or group of individuals, there will be some areas in which they are fairly competent at solving problems, other areas in which they can solve them without too much difficulty, and perhaps others in which they find great difficulty even keeping their heads above water. If assessment has covered a wide range of problem areas, it should be possible to construct, for each individual or for a group as a whole, a *profile* showing the pattern of these strengths and weaknesses. This can signal, in graphic form, areas of deficit or areas requiring attention, much more dramatically than perhaps counselling or some other methods might. It is possible that a pattern may emerge pointing to the true root of a set of apparently unrelated problems, or that shows certain strengths or advantages which could be used to overcome other areas of difficulty. Here is an example of a simple problem profile in the area of work.

	Not a problem for me	I can succeed if I try	I usually fail
1 Wanting a job			
2 Applying for jobs			
3 Being interviewed			
4 Settling in			
5 Getting on with workmates			
6 Getting on with supervisors			
7 Timekeeping			
8 Getting my rights			
9 Staying in jobs			
10 Developing skills			

On such a sheet, an individual is asked simply where he stands in relation to each of the items on the left; he then connects up all the points with a line and a profile of his strengths and weaknesses is obtained. This can then be used to draw out more specific objectives based on the informational, attitudinal, or skill elements he thinks he could change. Some kinds of assessment material, such as problem check lists, lend themselves very well to this form of interpretation.

SENTENCE COMPLETION

Many individuals will be able to think of objectives of certain kinds by using sentence completion. Ask them to complete some appropriate sentences, e.g.

By tomorrow afternoon I want to have . . .
What I most want to do about (this problem) is . . .

Next time this (situation) happens I will . . .
I want to . . .
To do (such-and-such) I will first of all need to . . .
My next step must be to . . .

You can ask a group to complete these sentences one or more times as the situation requires. Most people enjoy doing this and we have found that they are surprisingly direct in what they produce.

This kind of sentence-completion exercise can also be expanded to employ the type of table set out below. Individuals could be asked to try completing this table on their own or in pairs, for as many problems as they think fit.

Problem	Steps toward solving this problem could be . . .
My biggest problem is: 'losing jobs through being late for work'	going to bed earlier, drinking less, buying a reliable alarm clock, getting a job that interests me . . .
I also have problems with: 'drinking too much'	going out later each evening, going out in a different group or to a different pub, taking less money with me, switching the kinds of thing I drink . . .
I also have problems with: '. . .'	. . .

CHECK LISTS OF SPECIMEN OBJECTIVES

If people have difficulty in thinking up specific objectives for themselves, it may be of help to give them a list of someone else's objectives (with their permission of course), or a list that you have made up, and ask them which of these they think *they* could make objectives of their own. With a long list you can ask them to tick, or put a circle round, the objectives they would choose.

Such 'specimen' lists can be either specific, focussing on one area of relevance to a particular group, or very general, covering a whole range of areas. It is usually best if some variety is introduced, with only a majority of items from the key area – the real problem may lie elsewhere, anyway, e.g. a man drinks because he cannot find anything else to do with his time. Here is a five-item check list on one topic, that of citizens' rights:

☐ 1 I need to know more about tenancy laws.
☐ 2 I need to be more firm with sales people.

☐ 3 I would like to understand X's views on abortion.
☐ 4 I wish I could hold my temper when I'm complaining.
☐ 5 I am going to write to my M.P. about this.

Individuals would be simply asked to mark which of these objectives they could adopt themselves; they might then want to rephrase them in their own way. Of course, a check list needs to be longer than this to cover individual needs in a small group; nevertheless we have found that, with a 135-item check list of a general nature, individuals (in groups between four and twelve in size) will happily mark off between twenty and sixty items. The key to all of this is to make your own check list suited to the needs of the individuals you will be working with.

COUNSELLING

This is a traditional method of helping individuals make decisions about goals. It may be conducted in a number of ways. The normal pattern is where the counsellor, usually a trained professional, possibly in a specialized area (e.g. careers, marriage) works on a one-to-one basis with an individual. Alternatively, individuals with common problems may share their views on them, and try from their different perspectives to counsel each other ('co-counselling'). Ideally, counselling involves a number of basic qualities, the chief aim of which is the development of an understanding *relationship* between the parties involved. This involves the building up of trust and empathy, the conquering of interpersonal anxieties and 'blocks' of an emotional kind, and the giving by the counsellor of various kinds of (usually emotional) support to the person in his hour of need. Counselling is a subtle process, but there is in it a danger of drifting away from common sense into emotional complexities which can exacerbate rather than relieve the existing problems. On the other hand there are many situations in which all individuals need is to know that someone else agrees with them, shares their view of something, or supports them in a plan of action. In this sense counselling may be indispensable to many forms of personal change.

PEER INTERVIEWS

The problem-solving table on page 64 may prove too difficult to be completed thoroughly in peer interviews and may need wider discussion to produce the final result. However, a start may well be made (using the table as a framework for the task) by pairing people off, and asking them to interview each other and to come away after ten to fifteen minutes with a list of at least some of the other person's problems and the steps that might be necessary for their solution. Some tentative objectives may also emerge in the process.

WALL CHARTS AND MATRICES

These are a more 'extraverted' method of enabling individuals to crystallize their goals for themselves, in so far as they involve writing down (possibly for display to a group as a whole) personal goals in a particular way. All that this involves is asking individuals to fill in some boxes in a matrix on a sheet of paper; what exactly the boxes have to contain is a decision that is up to group members. Some examples might make this clearer.

In one kind of wall sheet, individuals are asked to fill in boxes with changes they would like to make, by saying what they would like 'more' of or 'less' of during a given time period. The areas chosen can be anything at all.

Objectives – next six months	I need more of	I am happy	I need less of
At Work			
At Home			
Self			
Leisure			

Objectives – next six months	+++	– – –	Practical goals
School			
Hobbies			
Friends			

In another method, individuals can be asked to identify strengths and weaknesses (or 'plusses' and 'minusses') in selected areas, together with some practical goals they could set in a given time period.

There are many variations that can be made on this: the topics down the left-hand side can be named or left up to individuals; small or large sheets can be used; individuals can be asked to put them up on the wall, or exchange them with particular people, or take them home; or the categories along the top can also be varied. In general, a great deal will depend on the group atmosphere – whether or not individuals are prepared to commit themselves to paper. The exercise works best with a group that is committed to problem solving, amongst whose members a fair degree of openness exists; it can then be a quite entertaining and extremely useful approach to setting objectives.

LADDER SCALES

A simpler but perhaps even more individualistic method of helping individuals to think about the personal goals they might set consists of asking them to imagine themselves positioned on a ladder which in some way represents their life. At the bottom of the ladder is 'rock bottom' – representing the state (which they themselves are asked to describe) that was the worst they have ever been in: their 'all-time low'. This could be outlined in financial, physical, emotional, social, or other terms – depending entirely on the individuals. At the top of the ladder is the opposite state – the one they would really like to be in, with all the attributes of personal happiness as they see it. This could of course be entirely utopian and unrealistic, but in the main individuals tend to describe a state which, though very difficult for them to arrive at, could nevertheless be realized if appropriate action were taken.

Individuals are then asked to do two things. First, they are asked to enter on the ladder – which might generally consist of ten to twelve steps – where they are *now* in relation to each of these states. They can enter this at any point on the ladder. Second, they are then asked to specify, being as realistic as possible, the things they would need to do to get higher on the ladder – as near the top as possible if not actually on it. The steps derived from doing these can then be used as, or transformed into, personal objectives for the near and long-term future.

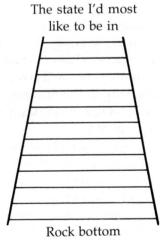

The state I'd most
like to be in

Rock bottom

This exercise proves most useful when used in conjunction with the lifelines or 'snakes' of the assessment chapter; individuals are asked to look first at where they have come from and then at where they are going. This is a fairly natural progression of thought – and provides us with a new kind of 'snakes and ladders' game.

GROUP DISCUSSION

Yet another method of helping individuals and groups to set personal (or joint) objectives is that of group discussion. This ubiquitous element of problem solving is as useful here as at other stages of the process, in providing feedback and second opinions, clarifying or encouraging remarks, or simply a public venue for the objective-setting process. Commitment to a course of action in public is a strong encouragement to carry out that action; and, in general, the group discussion helps to lubricate the actions of the process as a whole.

BRAINSTORMING AND PATTERN NOTES

These two techniques, which have been described in the assessment chapter, can also be used for setting objectives. When brainstorming, everyone's initial thoughts on personal objectives could be listed quickly as a stimulus. Using pattern notes, individuals could make a general objective the central core and work outwards with subsidiary or short-term objectives.

The final stages of setting objectives

It was suggested earlier that the writing down of objectives often helps to make their attainment slightly easier. Some objectives will be general; some will probably require being broken down into smaller steps towards the achievement of a more major goal. Yet others will take the form of short-term, small-scale targets. A written document will allow the individual to record both his overall plan and the specific objectives within it, and will enable him to monitor what progress he is making towards them. It will also act as a guide during the learning phase of the process, indicating activities which are likely to be useful.

Some individuals find it helpful to call such a written statement of objectives a 'contract' in which they undertake to do specified things within specified time limits. Staff members add their own undertakings to the document and everybody who is a party to the document signs it. We do not suggest that this should be done by everyone as a matter of course during the problem-solving process. It may be sufficient for an individual to formulate a private resolve to do something, which he never divulges to anyone else. He may want to talk to a fellow group member or a staff member. He may want to write something down in response to an incomplete sentence, or on prepared forms of varying degrees of complexity. Or he may not. The choice is his to do whatever seems best at the time.

Methods of setting objectives are summarized in the table – a section out of the 'curriculum matrix' – shown below.

Setting objectives: section of the curriculum matrix

Setting objectives	Check lists of specimen objectives, profiles of problem areas, sentence completion, wall charts, brainstorming and pattern notes, counselling and co-counselling, group discussion

Note: See page 139 for the completed curriculum matrix

The process of setting objectives

This last section of this chapter looks at a process for setting objectives. If objectives have not appeared spontaneously, and the methods just outlined do not seem to be working well, it may be necessary to formalize the process a little more, and to help individuals or groups through it in a series of stages. The scheme below outlines four simpler stages of the objective-setting process, some of which draw upon methods described in the previous section.

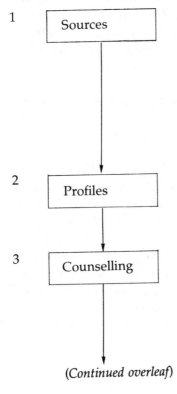

1   **Sources**

Information generated in the assessment stage is pooled and surveyed in global terms, with information from:
- formal pencil-and-paper sources
- unstructured pencil-and-paper methods
- interviews
- observations
- group behaviour/group discussions
- external sources.

2   **Profiles**

Using these sources, it should be possible to focus on areas requiring attention, and to do this with successively greater fineness on profile sheets like the one outlined in the previous section.

3   **Counselling**

It should then be possible to work with groups or individuals to answer some basic questions. Focussing on the assessment profiles, decisions can be made about which areas to work on, and the *kinds* of change identified that have to be made, e.g. in knowledge, experience, attitude, interest, skill, feeling, confidence, habits, and so on.

(Continued overleaf)

4

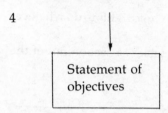

Statement of
objectives

Finally, some agreement can be reached for taking action. It might be best if this is written down or possibly made public; it could even be sealed, to be reopened at a given point in the future. Where possible the criteria for having carried it out successfully should be identified.

Individuals should now have lists of their problems, of steps by which these problems can be solved, and of concrete objectives which they have set themselves in relation to these steps. Whether or not *any* of this is made known to others is of course, ultimately, the prerogative of the individuals concerned. But, public or private, general or specific, one or many, the objectives that have now been set form the basis for action towards the solution of problems. This is the domain of 'learning', and it is to this that we turn in the next chapter.

Notes and references

The idea of setting behavioural objectives has come from learning theory and the practice of programmed instruction; but its uses have spread widely into many areas of education and therapy, where it often forms the basis of 'contracts' of various kinds.

An early text in the field of education is B. S. Bloom (1956) *Taxonomy of Educational Objectives: 1. Cognitive Domain* (New York: David McKay), and it was followed by the later handbook by B. S. Bloom, D. R. Krathwohl, and B. B. Masia (1964) *Taxonomy of Educational Objectives: 2. Affective Domain* (New York: Donald McKay).

A more recent, and prolific, writer on the business of formulating learning objectives is R. F. Mager. See, for example, his (1972) *Goal Analysis* (Belmont, California: Fearon). References to his other work will be found in this book.

In social work, Reid and Epstein have emphasized the importance of the 'client's' own perception of the problem and the specification of a task to be tackled within a given number of sessions: W. J. Reid and L. Epstein (1972) *Task Centered Casework* (New York: Columbia University Press). For an account of work with these methods in this country see M. Goldberg, D. Walker, and J. Robinson (1977) Exploring the Task-Centred Casework Method, *Social Work Today* **9** (2), 6 September. The idea of contracts is developed more fully in J. M. Hutten (1977) *Short Term Contracts in Social Work* (London: Routledge and Kegan Paul). And B. Hopson describes a complete procedure for helping individuals make decisions about their future lives, in Personal Re-evaluation: A Method for Individual Goal Setting, a chapter in J. Adams, J. Hayes, and B. Hopson (1977) *Transition: Understanding and Managing Personal Change* (London: Martin Robertson). See also the chapter on The Formation of Contract in T. Douglas (1976) *Groupwork Practice* (London: Tavistock).

5 Learning: methods and procedures

To a certain extent, the title of this chapter is a misnomer. It will probably be obvious by now that a safe and clear-cut categorizing of all the methods that are available for personal change is simply not possible. Everywhere there are overlaps, perhaps nowhere more evident than when we try to characterize learning procedures, for learning is taking place at every phase of the four-stage process. In assessment and self-assessment, individuals and groups discover strengths and weaknesses, explore new areas of self-knowledge, and acquire a great deal of information that may not have been available or seemed relevant before. When setting objectives, individual or group preferences become more marked, decisions are taken, and commitments are expressed. The introspection that accompanies – or motivates – personal change can produce its crucial transformations at any stage of the process, and might do so when we least expect it. We are saddled, therefore, with some kind of demand for an answer to the question: what distinguishes 'learning' as a stage of the process from any other?

It is possible, however, to sidestep this untidy problem, by saying simply this: any activities – group or individual, formal or spontaneous – that enable us to achieve the objectives we have set out in the preceding stages we call *learning procedures*. The rich and varied harvest of methods that emerges is testimony to the value of thinking in this way. Formal classes or training courses – to learn to read, to drive, to operate a machine; informal conversation or correspondence with other groups or individuals on any topic whatsoever; individual or community projects of a hundred-and-one kinds; the changing of habits or behaviour in any particular direction; the acquisition of skills, information, or insights, by teaching, counselling, role-playing, or practice; the achievement of any personal goals, regardless of the time scale involved – all can be used, without prejudice as to their source, during this stage of the process.

In fact, the vast majority of things that individuals do to achieve particular goals probably involve learning in the more conventional sense. Any personal change involves, at a minimum, the recognition of changes in oneself, and, more often than not, a development of part of the ability to bring about that change again in other settings. So, for present purposes, we want to use the word 'learning' in the broadest possible sense, stretched as far as imagination will allow. Anyone taking a cursory glance through the contents of this chapter should not be deceived, therefore, by the early appearance of direct teaching; less formal (and much less familiar) methods are surveyed in the pages that follow.

Chapter aims

The aims of this chapter are, therefore:

1 to survey a variety of methods used in learning;
2 to illustrate some practical uses of these methods, and suggest others;
3 to elaborate on the concept of problem solving and on related ideas, which are at the core of the approach of the book.

To help to organize the ideas and methods we shall be discussing, we can again use the threefold division of *kinds* of change that was introduced earlier, and on which the curriculum matrix is based: those of *knowing*, *feeling*, and *doing*. While many kinds of learning naturally sit astride these categories, they are indispensable as an anchor when we are faced with the sheer abundance of possibilities that learning procedures present.

Three kinds of change in learning

Knowing

Learning that involves finding new information, or learning to think in new ways.

   This is what is referred to when we use words and phrases such as 'find out', 'inform', 'memorize', 'understand', 'comprehend', 'look at in a new way', 'conceptualize', and so on.

Feeling

This is where learning involves changes in attitudes or emotions.

   It could be contained in words such as 'realize', 'express', 'counsel', 'grow', 'mature', 'motivate', 'influence', 'pressurize', 'tolerate', and many more.

Continued on following page

Doing
Where learning involves the performance of some action, or the development of some skill.
    This is represented in words like 'act', 'solve', 'decide', 'survive',
'manipulate', 'perform', 'execute'.

The survey of methods which forms the bulk of the chapter is organized along
the lines of this threefold division, bolstered where possible by actual examples of
methods that can be used. The biggest concentration of examples is in the *doing* area,
a result partly of their value in a social skills and personal problem-solving approach,
and partly of their likely unfamiliarity compared with the other two groups of
methods.

Methods of learning

KNOWING

Methods of acquiring new information derive mainly from the arena of education –
where this can mean anything from teaching in a school to the screening of a documen-
tary film on TV; but there are a number of other sources too. For convenience we can
classify *knowing* methods under five major headings, before looking at each one in
turn:

    1 direct teaching methods
    2 self-organized learning
    3 materials used in vocational guidance
    4 brainstorming techniques
    5 group discussion.

1 *Direct teaching* or 'didactic' methods are those in which information, in the hands (or
more likely the head) of one individual or group, is transferred to those of another by
some means: by word of mouth, printed page, audiovisual aids, or even through the
mass media. The colossal variety within such methods themselves almost defies
description, and more are made available almost every day. The day when we can
learn anything by connecting up our brains to a computer may not be too far distant;
until it arrives perhaps we can use some of the methods outlined in the accompanying table.

Some direct teaching methods
- Face-to-face methods such as formal lectures, less formal talks, tutorials, seminars, and other forms of personal contact.

- The use of printed materials in books, leaflets, catalogues, newspapers, magazines, journals, maps, plans, flow charts.

- The addition of audiovisual aids, from flipcharts and boards to scale models, slides, films, overhead projectors, audio- and video-tape.

- Visits to places of interest.

- Broadcasts on radio or TV, records, telephone tutorials.

Almost any form of learning is likely to incorporate one or other of these methods at some stage. Most personal problems involve an information deficit of some kind, which can sometimes be put right simply by telling individuals the relevant facts, handing them the appropriate leaflet, or sending them along to the most suitable address. If one person wants to know something another already knows, the simplest possible form of learning can take place directly, by word of mouth.

Of course, the majority of these methods are almost universal (most people are exposed to them in school) and their forceful presence, both there and, more pervasively, in the media, makes them almost contemptible in their familiarity. There can be little doubt, however, that they are under-used in many of the 'helping' professions such as social work and residential care. The sheer imparting of a necessary diet of facts is often neglected where people with problems are concerned.

One simple direct teaching tool that can be very useful in rectifying this is the *hand-out* – a specially prepared leaflet summarizing some essential information on a topic of concern. We tend to associate the term 'hand-outs' with the dry reading lists distributed on college courses, or with all too easily ignored pamphlets distributed by pressure groups. A good hand-out need not be dry; nor need it be thrown away unread in case it might unsettle us. By combining a clear-cut heading announcing its area of concern, an associated picture or story that catches the eye, and a simple statement of the information required, hand-outs can be of inestimable value in supplying data for the solution of problems. The example on page 75 gives an (admittedly limited) illustration of the sort of thing that can be done, in one problem area. With a moment's thought, you could easily improve on this.

The business of giving direct information seems daunting to most people – for fear, perhaps, that others might take them for 'experts'. Nevertheless, the skills involved are

Alcohol and the body

The active ingredient of the alcoholic drinks we consume is called <u>ethyl alcohol</u>. Although it can be made artificially in a laboratory, in the main it is produced through the fermentation, by yeast, of the naturally-occurring sugars found in plants.

WHY PUB GRUB CAN BE SUCH A YAWN

By Robert Millar

If you fancy a pie and a pint this lunchtime, think again.

For the traditional pub lunch, far from being nutritious and stimulating, could be to blame for the tiredness and lack of concentration that affects many office workers in the afternoon.

The reason, says Professor Vincent Marks, of Surrey University, is that consumption of a moderate dose of alcohol with mainly carbohydrate foods leads to sugar deficiency in the blood.

Headaches

In tests at the university clinical chemistry department, blood glucose levels in some volunteers fell so low that they suffered headaches and impaired work performance.

The medical explanation seems to be that alcohol and carbohydrate foods help to release insulin into the bloodstream too quickly.

Commenting on the findings, the British Nutrition Foundation says: "The quantity of alcohol and sugar given to the volunteers was equal to three double gin-and-tonics.

"The effect on work performance and safety has still to be assessed."

Reproduced by kind permission of the *Daily Express* newspaper (printed 17 January 1978, Manchester edition).

After being swallowed, alcohol is absorbed into the bloodstream through the linings of the stomach and intestines, and passes to all the tissues of the body. Gradually it is broken down into carbon dioxide and water, save for a small amount which passes out in the breath or in the urine.

Though alcohol may have some effects on the heart rate and possibly influence other organs, its chief effect is on the nervous system, the system that organizes movement and co-ordination, attention, perception, and memory.

Its effect is to depress the functioning of the nervous system. This means it acts a bit like an anaesthetic affecting speech, balance, judgement, making us less sensitive to pain, slowing our reaction times, and eventually rendering us unconscious.

Prolonged ingestion of large amounts of alcohol can have more serious bodily effects. These include anorexia (disturbance of appetite), gastritis (inflamed stomach), cirrhosis (a disease of the liver), and amnesia (acute loss of memory). Withdrawal from a high level of alcohol consumption can cause delirium tremens (DTs), hallucinations, and epileptiform fits.

The effects of alcohol on the nervous system depend on its concentration in the bloodstream. This concentration is usually recorded in milligrams of alcohol per one hundred milliletres of blood (abbreviated mg%). The table below illustrates some effects at different concentrations of blood alcohol.

40mg%:	two drinks; most people start to feel relaxed
60mg%:	judgement is impaired; people over-estimate their capabilities
80mg%:	definite impairment of co-ordination, e.g. in driving
100mg%:	legally drunk in many countries
120mg%:	vomiting occurs unless this level is reached slowly
150mg%:	balance and movement impaired (nearly three-quarters of a bottle of whisky in the blood)
300mg%:	many people lose consciousness
450mg%:	breathing stops: DEATH

fairly simple ones – whichever of the above methods may be used. (Some comments on this point are made in Chapter 9.)

2 *Self-organized learning methods* perform a very similar job to didactic methods – with the difference that the learner himself becomes the controller of the process, regulating its speed, quality, and direction. Some of the methods involved are listed in the table.

Methods for self-organized learning
– Programmed learning from texts or machines.
– Individualized learning packages for particular groups of people, or particular topics or problems.
– Projects: carried out either by individuals, e.g. when on a course of some kind, or by groups, e.g. as part of a community development programme.

Materials of this kind are available from many sources and cover topics ranging from the actual work content of many jobs to information about such diverse subjects as home repairs or procedures for solving personal problems. We shall take a closer look at just one of these methods, programmed learning.

Programmed. learning is based on principles derived from behaviouristic learning theory. Basically, it is a method of self-instruction in which the physical presence of the tutor has been replaced by a written text or teaching machine; the real tutor has prepared the material along programmed lines. The essence of programmed learning is that the material to be learned is arranged in a manner that, for that kind of material, results in the most effective learning. The key features on which most programme writers are agreed are:

1 the material to be learned is broken down into small steps which are carefully sequenced;
2 the learner is asked to make overt responses, usually by answering questions set at the end of each learning step;
3 the learner is given immediate feedback about the accuracy of his reply: he has usually to provide the correct answer before he can go on to the next step;
4 the pace of the action is then under the control of the learner.

Quite simply, then, a book or machine presents information in a question-and-answer form, with progress through the material being dependent upon giving correct answers; it is assumed that this 'reward' process makes for more effective learning. Two main kinds of programme exist, distinguished by the style of response required of the learner.

1 The *'constructed-response' type* requires the learner to write in an answer, often in the form of sentence completion, and the material as a whole is arranged in linear fashion.
2 The *'multiple-choice' kind*, on the other hand, asks the learner to select one from a group of alternative answers to a question set at the end of each step. The material is arranged in a complex set of branches, and the particular branch which the learner takes is determined by his response.

The early use of programmed learning texts, which adhered to a rigid set of principles, has now largely given way to a range of self-teaching methods characterized by a 'multi-media' approach – for example in the combination of a 35 mm strip projector with an audio-cassette tape-recorder.

Programmed learning is, however, a highly formalized self-teaching technique. *Individualized learning packages*, by contrast, can combine formal and informal learning methods in varying balance, determined by the needs of some particular group. Most flexible of all amongst the self-teaching approaches, however, are *projects*, in which individuals not only decide the area they want to work on, but also determine how they will do so, and produce the materials required. Some potential aims of projects might be:

to carry out an opinion poll on a controversial topic

to conduct a survey of needs or resources in a local area

to 'research' some topic of interest and compile a report on it

to produce a leaflet or booklet of facts on some recognized problem

to compile an agenda for a series of discussions, or for community action

to prepare a learning package for use by someone else.

Self-organized learning methods have the advantage that they feed on themselves, and can be used to nourish one another in innumerable ways: for instance, one group of individuals can embark on a project to produce materials which another can use for learning purposes, as suggested in the last example above.

Considering the efficacy of some self-organized learning, it has been relatively little used; perhaps the most widely dispersed material are those used in some areas of literacy teaching, but even these offer scope for expansion.

An interesting illustration of the combined use of direct and self-teaching methods is provided by the *learning exchange*. This is a relatively recent development on the educational front which is experiencing considerable growth in the United States, and in this country to a more limited extent. In a learning exchange, individuals living in a given area register as being interested in teaching a given subject, through a central bureau or index; others who wish to learn can consult the index for teachers in the area of their choice. This is a departure from the traditional extramural or evening-class model in that it is organized directly by the community, and is completely open-ended; and since teacher and learner are doing it because they want to, it can be virtually free!

3 *Materials used in vocational guidance*, while to a certain extent forming a basis for careers counselling (outlined below under *Feeling*), also involve the imparting of a great deal of information, and can be used without the counselling element. They are materials organized in a particular way – usually sets of cards or specially produced books – which incorporate cross-indexing systems that will enable individuals to discover more about jobs in which they are interested, or identify job areas in which they *might* be interested. One such set of materials is described below.

Vocational guidance materials: Signposts
This set of cards was prepared by the Careers and Occupational Information Centre for use in schools; it is, however, equally useful for anyone changing careers, or deciding to train for a career late in life.

Essentially, *Signposts* is a boxed set of cards divided up into ten broad areas of interest:

Scientific	*Social Service*	*General Service*
Literary	*Artistic*	*Persuading/Influencing*
Computational	*Practical*	*Nature*
	Outdoor/Active	

On a card at the front of each category is a set of questions about the individual's interests. At the front of the scientific category, for example, the card reads: 'Are you interested in knowing the how and why of things, particularly in the realm of science?'. A list of possible careers in this category is then given, e.g. air traffic control, chiropodist, engineer, home economist, ophthalmic optician, physicist. If the person seeking advice and information has little or no idea of what he wishes to do, he can quickly read through all ten category heading cards, noting any to which his answer would be 'yes'. He can then look at the cards within any section, making a note of any card that describes an occupation that seems interesting. Each card then directs him, via a library classification number, to a standard section of a careers library. The card also lists more general books, pamphlets, and addresses for those who have no access to a careers library. Naturally not every job is represented, but there is a very wide selection. A supplementary set of cards lists careers connected with particular academic subjects.

The kinds of information to which such materials give access include basic job descriptions: what jobs involve on a day-to-day basis, the career structures in various occupations, entry requirements and opportunities for training, and sources of further information or actual openings. Inevitably, unskilled occupations are for the most part excluded. However, for most other jobs, from the semi-skilled to the top-level managerial, useful information can be made available in a readily digestible form.

4 *Brainstorming techniques* – dealt with initially under assessment – are also key methods in the learning process. They differ radically, however, from the methods we have discussed so far. They draw on our capacities for divergent thinking, the exploratory and imaginative kind of thinking whose role is so crucial in creative problem solving. They allow us to leap across boundaries, to tame our irrational ideas, to consort with disorder and put it to organized use. Rather than provide specific answers to particular questions, they throw out new questions and a hundred answers to each. In essence, they are keys for unlocking doors, and letting ideas flow: the means of generating information from within our own heads, which later we can match up to the outside world.

The basic notion of *brainstorming* has been introduced in the chapter on assessment. By suspending judgement, freewheeling, producing ideas in quantity, and looking for connections between them, we can produce many more ideas on any given topic than would be possible with our normal stop-go method of thinking. Such a process lends itself eminently well to learning and solving problems, and various techniques of brainstorming prove equally fruitful for doing just this.

The *'5W–H' system*, for example, can be applied as easily to the business of problem solving as to assessment, for generating numerous ideas on ways to make changes of any kind, particularly when focussed on the question 'How?'.

Pattern notes, which we also encountered during assessment, are just as useful again in the area of learning. They can be adapted by simply changing the word or phrase placed at the centre of the pattern; for example, we could do pattern notes on:

House improvements

A better use of my time

Changes I could make in . . .

Ways of . . .

Brainstorming methods are primarily intended for use with groups, and may be at their most fruitful when many heads combine to solve a problem together; pattern notes, however, lend themselves equally well to individual use, and can be applied also

An example of pattern notes used in problem solving

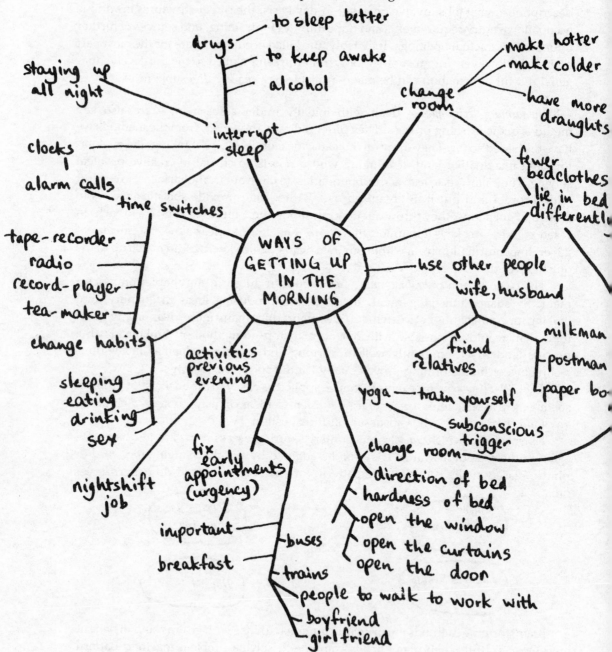

to the processes of note-taking and memorizing – important aspects of any changes in the *knowing* area.

5 *Group discussion* becomes ubiquitous during the application of the approach outlined in this book. Most people need no encouragement to talk about their own problems: when involved in sets of activities designed to help them solve those problems, everything within reach becomes a topic for discussion, a focus of group attention from which something of value can be gleaned. The group discussion is a forum for the exchange of information, the expression of views, and the clarification of opinion and belief, not to mention the development and maintenance of the life of a group. As a mode of learning even academic subjects, there is evidence to suggest that it is at least as effective a medium as the formal lecture, and highly preferable to it in other respects. It is not uncommon to discover individuals who, though they might recoil with horror from the prospect of formally addressing a group, will prove rich sources of experience and funds of useful comment in a setting of free discussion. In arriving at a balanced picture of the information available on any topic, the group discussion is unsurpassed; we shall be looking at some of its other merits when we come to the area of *feeling*. Possibly more than any other method, the group discussion cuts across our learning categories – if only because the solution of problems or the making of decisions involves the examination of facts and feelings as they exist for most of us – as inextricably intertwined threads in the fabric of our experience.

The five methods – or groups of methods – that we have been discussing are the principal means by which learning of the *knowing* variety can be brought about. These methods vary greatly in formality, in the demands they make on learners, in the degree of learner participation they make possible, and, on more practical lines, in the kinds and costs of resources necessary to make them work. The majority of them are, however, within the reach, directly or indirectly, of most workers in the helping agencies; so much so that a lot of choice and variety could be provided for the customers of such agencies in attempting to solve problems that stem from lack of information. In the next section we look at some quite different learning procedures, those we can use in the 'feeling' and attitudinal area.

FEELING

Methods of changing the way individuals feel towards something (including themselves), and of enabling them to change their attitudes, are drawn predominantly from psychotherapy and its many diverse areas of influence, though certain kinds of organizational training have also made substantial contributions. Some methods, like specific forms of groupwork, are very obviously 'therapeutic' in origin; others, like vocational counselling, owe more diffuse debts to therapy, and seem generally to have emerged from some sort of concern with the 'self concept' – in emphasizing self-awareness, self-evaluation, self-esteem, and self-control. We can divide the methods into four principal sorts:

1 counselling methods
2 group discussion
3 role-play of various kinds
4 groupwork and confrontation methods.

1 *Counselling methods*: As a learning method, counselling is intended primarily for use with individuals rather than groups; it provides a direct personal means of coming to terms with a whole variety of problems. In the most general sense, counselling is carried out daily in the community by parents, friends, doctors, and priests, the key aspects of the process being trust and empathy, which, when built up, enable individuals to accept help in making decisions that are realistic, and in following attainable courses of action.

A certain mystique has grown up around counselling, the effect of which has been to obscure what is essentially a simple process – one that can be put to use by anyone. Counselling can be, and should be, both practical *and* effectively related to immediate problems in personal relationships, task performance, and professional and personal development. There are three major kinds of counselling for use in personal problem solving: personal counselling, vocational counselling, and co-counselling.

Personal counselling
This form of counselling can be used effectively as a learning method with emotional, attitudinal, and interpersonal types of problem. The structure of such a counselling session would basically consist of:

(a) development of trust and communication: this 'establishment of rapport' can be built up with open-ended questions, a friendly manner and atmosphere, and a willingness to listen;
(b) gathering of information, by encouraging free and relevant talk on the problem area;
(c) promotion of understanding: helping the individual to see why he feels or acts in a certain way, by providing suggestions for comment and consideration;
(d) making decisions: the individual makes decisions which have been extracted from a number of alternative solutions that have been previously raised and discussed. A recapitulation of what has been achieved, and of anything that now needs to be done, provides positive reinforcement.

This form of counselling can be carried out by anyone, and often has a value for the individual that would not come from other methods.

Vocational counselling

Though often regarded as a professional or semiprofessional process, this need not be so. Help can often be obtained from schools or local authority careers officers; the overall aim is simply matching capabilities to opportunities, taking an individual's personality into account. What individuals are capable of will have been established during the assessment stage, and the counselling process represents both an information-giving and 'coming-to-terms' form of learning. Here, the individual can relate psychological information (on aptitudes, interests, and skills, and social factors – for example, about environmental and family influences) to opportunities in the job market and the world of work as a whole. As with personal counselling, the overall aim is to help the individual solve a problem – in this case relating to work – in as non-directive a manner as possible.

Co-counselling

Co-counselling can be seen as the learning equivalent of peer interviews, in this case giving individuals opportunities to counsel each other on problems in which they have some shared experience. It can be a formalized process following the steps outlined under 'personal counselling' above, or simply an informal exchange of ideas. If it is to be used extensively, or if individuals wish to take away with them the ability to help other people with their problems, then it might be a good idea to organize some basic instruction in counselling skills (through a talk, a hand-out, some video exercises, or group discussion). The basic assumption is that anyone can be a counsellor and can effectively help others.

Apart from making decisions about work, the kinds of problem for which counselling methods are likely to prove most useful are those that relate in some way to an individual's personal life: marriage and family problems, anxiety and learning to handle it, emotional difficulties of many kinds, interpersonal conflicts and misunderstandings, and decisions, for example, about whether or not to have a child, whether to move away from the home area, on how to cope with a handicapped relative, and many more.

2 *Group discussion methods* must be given high priority amongst methods of promoting change and solving problems in the *feeling* area. We have already touched on the importance of group discussion at the assessment stage, and have also pointed to its value as a method of acquiring information – as a kind of 'verbal learning exchange'. It certainly seems to be the case that group learning based on intensive free discussion leads to a greater understanding of concepts and principles when compared with more

traditional ways of teaching any kind of subject matter, from the laws of physics to the understanding of behaviour in groups. But the ever-present nature of group discussion as part of the whole problem-solving process lends to it additional advantages with significant pay-offs in the *feeling* area.

First, group discussion has a great impact on the level of *motivation* of members of a group. The presence of other people with similar problems which they wish to tackle is a powerful motivating factor for individuals in any learning context. This is a principle that has been exploited by self-help groups, and is being used increasingly in higher education. The surrender of control by leaders of groups to their members can greatly enhance the learning atmosphere, and lead to a markedly improved work rate; it certainly leads to greater enjoyment and satisfaction on the part of group members – which, even if they had no perceptible effect on group performance, would be a valuable bonus in the learning process.

Second, group discussion affords considerable opportunities for learning from the *shared experience* of group members. At its simplest this reflects the way in which most people acquire the bulk of their information, values, and attitudes in real life – from other people, by listening to conversation, watching television, or reading the printed word in innumerable places. In group discussion this process can be accelerated and intensified, and focussed more sharply on specific topics. One by-product of prolonged exposure to group discussion is a greater awareness of others and their predicaments, and a greater ability to understand their attitudes and beliefs in relation to one's own.

This brings us to the third, and possibly the most valuable, benefit of the group discussion approach to learning: that of *insight*. Even when a conversation is directed towards external problems such as money, drink, or offending behaviour, participation implies the exposure of an individual's views and experiences to the scrutiny of others, in a way that is not typical of everday life. The result is an enhanced appreciation of the self in relation to others; a deeper understanding, for the individual, of why he is as he is; and a stronger, yet more subtle, grasp of what his possible capabilities are. This psychotherapists have traditionally called 'insight'. But it can be achieved without the stresses, the provocations, or the manipulations of much contemporary psycho-therapy.

A final advantage of this method of learning is that of *mutual support*. In the right atmosphere, group membership fosters a willingness to work together, and to provide help for others, which can contribute much to the process of learning. This is not automatically true of all groups, nor of all members in any particular group. But it is true often enough, and generally enough, to say that it can be expected as one of the outcomes of normal group discussion methods in ordinary conditions.

While group discussion is, as we have said, a natural companion of problem solving, it can also be stimulated in other ways if need be. The use of cartoons depicting difficult situations like the one shown here, sharing the leading of discussions amongst

A cartoon discussion 'starter'

group members, or the structuring of discussions in more game-like ways can all be used to generate talk and action should they be held back for any other reasons.

3 *Role-play*, containing as it does a strong *doing* element, again fits less than perfectly into our threefold scheme of things, but since it contains a major component of 'taking the attitude of another' we can take time to look at it here. Role-playing is one of the most powerful tools in the whole spectrum of learning methods that this chapter surveys. In essence it is simple: individuals take parts in depicting some social event, large or small, real or imagined; and the nature of the event, its different possible outcomes, and the goings-on in the heads of various participants are explored, in an attempt to re-create the event as realistically as possible. The learning can derive from a number of sources: from the viewing of an event from different standpoints; from an increased awareness of the effects of actions on others; from a developing sense of the flexibility of interaction and an ability to anticipate and control its outcome; from the reversal of roles; and from the assimilation of any information, attitudes, and skills that may be the accompaniments of particular roles.

Done badly, role-playing can be trivial and artificial; the minimal benefits in this case will only be some mild form of entertainment. When taken more seriously, its effects can be singularly dramatic, not the least of them being general gains in confidence experienced over successive tries at it – gains which transfer to other social situations. An intriguing study by Philip Zimbardo has illustrated the potentially massive effects of role-play. Zimbardo asked his students (a psychology class in an American university) to take the parts of prisoners and guards in an extended role-play of life in prison. Members of both groups – provided with appropriate uniforms and briefings, and lodged in the basement of the psychology building – knew the situation was artificial and that they could opt out at any time; Zimbardo and his colleagues simply waited to see what would happen. The ensuing series of events, with occupants of both kinds of roles becoming rapidly absorbed within them, progressive deterioration of relationships between the two groups, and eventual near-riots, forced the termination of the role-playing experiment on the fifth day, as widespread violence threatened to engulf the whole scene. Yet at every stage the partners to the experiment had known it was a game, had 'known' who they really were; but they had somehow been taken prisoner – in a more fundamental sense – by their roles. Results like this leave the efficacy of role-play completely beyond question; for the participants in the experiment, it proved to be a learning experience of unparalleled power and value.

Though the method used by Zimbardo could hardly be adopted in education or social services (though the results might prove interesting), role-play can be used with great effect on a different scale. Role-plays have a number of elements, each of which can be structured to a different degree. In the most structured kind, parts can be allocated to those involved in the action, each with a distinct set of aims and expectations, and possibly even a script. Structured role-plays are extremely useful in rehearsing (or solving problems associated with) the many stereotyped situations we all confront at some time – like job interviews, negotiations at work, or dealings with officialdom wearing any of its many different hats. With a little thought and invention you can design many of these for yourself.

Less structured role-plays can be devised, however, to help individuals explore 'problem events' and deal with them in their own ways. These could be simple everyday situations familiar to most, for example:

introducing two people who do not know one another

asking someone to move from your seat in a pub

coping with someone who jumps a queue

buying contraceptives in a chemist's

asking for a day off work.

Alternatively they could be situations or events which are less common, and require greater subtlety of the participants:

handling aggression in a pub or discotheque

coping with a door-to-door salesman

refusing a request for a loan from someone who already owes you money

giving condolences to someone who has suffered a loss

resisting pressure from friends to drink, or commit an offence

making a complaint about goods in a shop, or service in a restaurant.

These are only the simplest of suggestions; for even less structured role-plays, it is possible to ask individuals themselves to describe scenes from their own past experience with which they coped badly, or which arouse regret about how they were handled. People can usually identify many situations that have gone wrong for them, which they have problems in negotiating, and which they would like to rehearse for future reference. Through role-play, the exploration of past and future events can become a learning experience for which no other could be substituted. In the next section (under *Doing*) we shall look at some other aspects of its use. Whatever the use being made of it, the maximum benefit can be derived here, as elsewhere, by rounding off a role-play session with group discussion of the salient points to have emerged from different individuals' points of view.

4 *Groupwork and sensitivity training methods* have undergone enormous growth in recent years; it would be possible to fill a chapter by just listing the names of the various approaches and techniques that are available. The methods they have fostered range from simple exercises that can be used on a one-off basis, to whole sets of activities produced by a given school of thought, which last for many sessions and demand considerable commitment from users. We can do little more here than refer to some of the more familiar developments that have been made, which include:

'Trust' exercises, which are used for establishing basic links between members of a group.

'Growth games', which are semi-structured exercises offering opportunities for increasing self-awareness and group affiliation. One is described on page 89.

Encounter and T-group methods, which are more involved and lengthy, and use a variety of 'sensitivity' training techniques.

Transactional analysis, a groupwork derivative of psychoanalytic theory that abounds in group and individual exercises, many of which can be used without any adherence to their theoretical underpinnings.

More esoteric approaches offering analyses of personality and individual change from a particular point of view, for example, Gestalt Therapy, Primal Therapy, Bio-energetics, and many more.

The majority of these methods or approaches have emerged from some of the points of intersection between psychoanalytic theory, recast as the therapist requires, and humanistic psychology, and particularly its manifestations in the 'human potential movement'. A number of sensitivity and T-group methods, however, have developed from work in organizational, and particularly management, training. In many cases, these methods require of users an almost complete absorption in one way of working, which can deprive users of the benefits of a varied approach to personal change, and when taken to extremes can in fact be stultifying and self-defeating. A further drawback on many of these approaches is that they violate the principle of *explicitness* as enunciated earlier in this book: they obfuscate the process of personal change by translating it into a specialized language – one consequence of which is the concentration of power in the hands of the therapist or group leader.

Our own suggestion, as with every other method outlined in this book, is to use at liberty any of the available methods as groups or individuals require: the sole criterion for the employment of any learning tool becomes its expected efficacy, its face value as a medium for change to the people who will be using it. While such theoretical agnosticism may be thought sacreligious in some quarters, we have found it pragmatic, appealing, and enjoyable.

A simple growth game

'Growth games' are based on the assumption that the potential of each individual for a full and enriching experience of themselves has to some extent been restricted by society. They attempt to overcome this by various means, which can range from actual physical exercises to more apparently game-like activities conducted by groups.

Many growth games aim at expanding social awareness, and we can look briefly at one here. Each member of a group is asked, in turn, to step outside the room. Remaining group members then write down something about the absent person – all on the same piece of paper (folding it over in turn so that others can not read what has been written). The absent group member then returns and is asked to try to identify the authors of the various remarks on the piece of paper. The game can produce interesting results – concerning how accurate individuals are in identifying authors; about the cues they use in doing so; about the different perceptions that emerge; and about the relation of these as a whole to their conception of themselves. The ensuing discussion can be fascinating, and (at the risk of occasional derogatory remarks – which should be discouraged initially) very enjoyable. It is best if this game is played by individuals who know each other to a certain extent. Its main drawback is time: up to fifteen minutes should ideally be allowed per group member.

A method of working which is common to many of these approaches to personal change is, paradoxically enough, that of *confrontation*. This involves the most direct, forceful presentation, to individuals or groups, of those aspects of problems that might be likely to 'disturb' them into action. In a way it is the equivalent of using photographs of lungs devastated by cancer to persuade people to stop smoking. As such, of course, this can be very effective. Confrontation may take the form either of facing individuals with some uncomfortable 'truths' about themselves, or of inducing dissonance in their beliefs by presenting to them facts that run counter to those beliefs. This obviously requires considerable care and calculation, and often no small amount of coercion.

Another kind of confrontation, however, occurs naturally in groups: the straightforward, frank, open kind of statement that is often made between individuals working towards a common goal. 'The trouble with you, John, is you talk too much.' Unlike the confrontation witnessed in many sensitivity-training groups, this need not be manipulative, requires no simulated anger or other emotion, and consists of little more than the giving, by one individual to another, of an opportunity to face an unpalatable fact. Most people can probably remember occasions when such advice had a beneficial effect.

One other interesting variant on the method of confrontation is described below. The confrontation in this case is with oneself; the method is called McFall's Mystical Monitor.

McFall's Mystical Monitor

This is a simple exercise in self-discovery. All you have to do is lock yourself up in a room with a tape-recorder, making sure you are entirely alone. First, talk into the tape-recorder on anything you wish, for about twenty minutes. Then play back the recording, and, having listened to it, make another recording, this time for at least half an hour. Play this back as often as you like, finally erasing all the evidence.

The common discovery of those who try this is that, despite the absence of an audience, they find themselves talking, at first, as if some audience were there. Later, as this illusion is dispelled, more basic issues, central to one's idea of oneself, begin to emerge. The only way to find out what this could mean is to try it.

The foregoing sets of learning methods are all aimed primarily at the 'feeling' area of learning – the area in which emotions and attitudes intermingle, and in which many 'personal' problems reside, in the sense in which this phrase is commonly understood. The use of these methods requires a great deal of care and openness to other people's points of view. There is no reason, however, why most of us should not become skilled in the use of them: as with most other kinds of problem, the most basic qualification for becoming involved in solving them is a willingness to help.

We have now surveyed the contents of two out of three of the 'boxes' formed by the curriculum matrix in the learning area: those of *knowing* and *feeling*. The next section completes the process, by looking into the third: that of *doing*.

DOING

An emphasis on *learning by doing* should be apparent throughout this book. For the majority of the problems with which 'common men' (and women) are faced, the solution invariably lies in taking action of some kind – in going to look for something (some information, a job, a place to live), in dealing with other people (in the DHSS, in the family, in court, at work), or in making a decision of some kind (about how to spend money or time, whether or not to drink, when to change jobs, whether to have children). Yet the educational and social agencies which mediate our adjustment to society have traditionally done little to foster the skills that are necessary for the performance of all these tasks. They are either learned informally, as in the majority of cases (though the anxiety which accompanies even the common job interview suggests they are not learned with much confidence) or – for a large minority – they are not learned at all. This section looks at some of the methods that can be used to help individuals acquire skills – *take-away skills* – for use across a wide range of situations that are pivotal to survival and adjustment in a society like ours.

These methods come from a wide range of sources: from education; from psychiatry; from management training; and from that more piecemeal strand of activity which might be loosely characterized as 'self-help' and whose aim has been to provide particular groups with the tools they needed for solving their problems more effectively. The methods can be divided up into:

1 social skills training methods
2 information-search, decision-making, and problem-solving exercises
3 simulations.

1 *Social skills training methods* are ways of enabling individuals to cope more effectively with social situations, by expanding their awareness of what goes on in social interaction, and furnishing opportunities to learn the skills involved in dealing with others. These skills might include the following:

expressing oneself
being aware of one's effect on others
self-assertion
self-control under provocation
resisting group pressure
understanding other people's intentions
being good at interviews.

Although some of these involve other than straightforward behavioural elements, it is often the case that the best way to learn them is by trying them out – first in constructed, and later in real, social situations.

Actually, the phrase 'social skills training' means different things to different people, the key difference being in what might be called the preferred 'unit of analysis'. Some trainers assert that a social skill must be broken down into its simplest elements – bodily movements, gestures, movements of eye, hand, and face – before it can adequately be improved. These elements are the ones that constitute the 'taken-for-granted' features of social interaction – in other words, we only become aware of them when they break down in some way. Others suggest that instead we can look at whole 'bits' of skill – like the handling of a complete social situation – and concentrate any training on

92 Social skills and personal problem solving

that. Since there are individuals who have problems that cut right across this distinction, it seems only fair to look briefly at them both.

Whatever the size of the piece of behaviour or skill we wish to develop, there are some elements of learning that cannot be dispensed with. These include *feedback*, *practice*, and *rehearsal*. A 'socially-skilled' performance is dependent for its effectiveness on the judgements of other people (we all have to learn such skills by testing out the reactions of others); similarly, effective training must provide individuals and groups with some feedback from others on how they are doing. Again, social skills are not – except on a few occasions – acquired without some experience of trial and error: as with learning to ride a bicycle or drive a car, practice makes perfect. Finally, not many of us are so suave and self-assured that we can cope with completely unexpected situations – the more we have prepared for some situation, and rehearsed it both behaviourally and in our imagination, the better our performance is likely to be.

Using these general methods at every stage of learning, we can look more closely at some specific methods that are available. They include:

basic exercises in the 'taken-for-granted' aspects of social skill
modelling
role-playing
successive approximation
analysis of critical incidents.

Basic social skills exercises would usually be suggested for individuals who have problems in the 'taken-for-granted' aspects of interaction, and whose social competence is impaired as a result. The consequences of this can be more serious than we might expect. Normal social intercourse depends on an intricate series of finely-tuned and well co-ordinated actions, involving posture, facial expression, gestures, eye contact, touch, and, of course, speech. There may be some relationship between deficiencies in these kinds of skills and some psychiatric illnesses; more frequently, exercises like these could be used as a source of help for what can be seen as 'clumsiness' in social interaction. Some examples are given below.

Some exercises in basic social skills

Personal space
Personal space is that area round individuals which they experience as their own – the invasion of which is felt as a threat, indication of intimacy, or other kind of personal approach.

A simple exercise can be used to bring this out. Ask two individuals to

---

stand, facing each other, about twelve feet apart; and then, slowly, to approach each other in short steps. When either feels that the other is close enough, he (or she) can ask the other to stop; and the distance between them (if any!) can be measured as an index of personal space. Apart from its obvious humorousness, the exercise can reveal something to people of which they were not aware.

The use of the voice: intonation
The modulation of voice tone is a characteristic feature of expressive ability – we all go to sleep when a monotone drones on. Individuals can practice using tone of voice by itself as a means of communication by addressing each other in numbers. Different tones of voice should emerge for different kinds of communication: asking and answering questions, giving a rebuke, giving condolences, issuing a command or a request. This exercise can be adapted to assessing how well individuals identify signals in tones; how well they use them themselves; and to learning by imitation. A tape-recorder might lessen the embarrassment in some cases.

Mapping touch areas of the body
The kind of communication that takes place through touch has particularly intimate qualities, and the pattern of which areas can be touched by which people – and in what way – is very complex indeed.

This could be explored by asking individuals which areas they feel they can legitimately touch on others, and which factors affect this: who the people are, the nature of the relationship, their sex and status, and the circumstances. It is actually possible to construct a map of the body indicating which areas are touchable by whom, and looking at differences between people in how they feel about this kind of contact with others.

Eye contact
During a normal conversation, individuals' eyes come into mutual contact only a certain proportion of the time. By watching two individuals engaged in conversation, and using a stopwatch, it is possible to discover some of the factors which influence how much of this 'mutual gaze' takes place. You can do this by varying the sex of the speakers, their distance apart, and the kind of conversation they are having. It is also worth considering the consequences of too much – or too little – eye contact during any encounter. What sort of impression does it leave us with?

In our view, the value of this kind of training and of what might be called the 'eyebrow' school of social skills training has been greatly over-emphasized. Most individuals with problems in this area can identify specific situations they have problems with, and the methods of training mentioned above are more applicable to these. Much more common than a breakdown in the supply of non-verbal cues is a more general feeling of inability to cope, probably arising from a variety of factors including unfamiliarity with some social situations, lack of confidence, inability to co-ordinate intentions with sequences of action, acting before thinking, and possibly lack of social insight and understanding of others. The rest of the methods in this chapter deal, therefore, with 'bigger bits' of social interaction, and often with whole incidents or events.

Modelling is the simplest and most straightforward of these. A great deal of the learning we all do in the course of growing up is based on the imitation of models; usually they have to be individuals to whom we are in some way attached for the learning to be at its most effective. People can, however, learn this way in later life, too – in cases where the actions in question are ones they themselves want to accomplish.

Modelling can be used in two principal ways in social skills training. First, many kinds of skilled action can be demonstrated by those who are skilled in them, to those who are not. A useful example of this, given in the box opposite, is using the telephone. Other examples might be:

apologizing to someone you have offended
asking somebody to dance
making a plea for yourself in court
asking a stranger for directions
picking up something someone has dropped and giving it to them.

These are very simple things to do; but some people have never done them. When shown how to do them, they can learn very rapidly; though the first attempt may be far from perfect, the groundwork has been laid for future improvements.

Second, modelling can also be used for more complex pieces of action. One application of this is the use of modelling to illustrate alternative ways of handling difficult incidents. If some incident is analysed in depth, it is virtually certain that some changes could have been made by participants in the way they acted. Those who suggest alternatives can be invited to describe them, and model them, before the group. The effect is less to provide behaviour for direct imitation than to illustrate the variety of ways in which any situation could be handled. Learning comes from a perception of this variety rather than the direct observation of one model.

Role-playing is central to social skills training; if individuals are to acquire more and better skills, receive useful feedback, or rehearse future action in some way, the best

Using the telephone

Using the telephone can serve as the prototype of the idea of a social skill. It is not an innate talent, but a learned piece of behaviour, usually acquired by tacit social learning methods. As with illiteracy, those who have failed to pick up the simple knack of making telephone calls are unlikely to advertise the fact, and will find ingenious means of avoiding the need ever to use the instrument. Also as with illiteracy, there is no socially acceptable way of acquiring this skill later in life. But it can be taught, directly, in a matter of minutes, so equipping the learner with a social skill of inestimable future value in all sorts of situation.

Coaching in the use of the telephone would consist simply of a run-through of the mechanics of making a call, followed by one demonstration (or more) of actual telephone use. The nearer the 'model' or demonstrator is in status to the learner, the more effective the learning; the best-possible tutor would be a fellow group member of the learner.

The principle of learning from the more competent can be employed in a group telephone-skills exercise. The group is divided into threes, each containing a caller, a listener, and an observer. The caller rings up the listener and holds a conversation for not more than two minutes on some pre-arranged topic. Suggested topics might be:

> ringing a firm about a job
> ringing a shop to complain about something
> ringing up an acquaintance to ask for a date.

The observer rates the caller's performance on a check list or rating scale of not more than ten items, covering, for example, the content of the call, its effectiveness, the manner of the performance, level of confidence, and so on.

The exercise can then be repeated with the individuals taking other roles, until each has, in turn, tried every role. Finally the exercise and the ratings should be discussed by each threesome and by the group as a whole.

possible route for them to take is by practising in role-play. Most people, after initial reluctance, become surprisingly good at role-play: some turn out to be stars. We have already looked at this method under *Feeling*; suffice it to say here that it is a basic component of all the kinds of training we are looking at in this section.

A useful variation on all of these techniques is to add to them the dimension of *successive approximation*. Despite such a daunting title this is really something quite simple. If some socially skilled act looks too difficult for us, we can try to handle it by making it easier. One way is to start with some action which is a poor relation of the one we are interested in and, over successive practice sessions, gradually to modify that behaviour so that it gets nearer and nearer – approximates towards – the target. Another is to divide the complex activity into simple parts and tackle each separately, then add them together one by one until, again, we are approximating the piece of behaviour which at first seemed so difficult. This may be making it sound easier than it is, but many kinds of social skills are acquired in this way. Successive approximation can also be used to help transfer the skills acquired in an artificial situation to perfor- mance in the real world beyond learning.

Critical incidents analysis is the most elaborate of social skills training methods, in that it is designed for the scrutiny of entire social events and their breakdown in as realistic a manner as possible. Situations that individuals have found difficult in the past, and may be confronted with again, are described, analysed, role-played, and examined closely with a view to formulating alternative courses of action. In a way they are a controlled version of what sometimes occurs when something goes wrong for us: it is replayed over and over again in the imagination, each time presenting us with something else we could have done, that would have made it all happen differently.

One kind of format that can prove useful in this respect is the 'action-replay', in which individuals are asked to imagine they are making a film about their own critical incident. The kinds of incident for which this would be suitable are extremely varied, but becoming involved in crucial arguments, making decisions hastily, committing offences, getting into fights, or not acting when one should have done are amongst the most obvious.

To make a film depicting an incident as it happened – in fact, using video, as film can be rather too expensive – requires a fairly penetrating analysis of an incident from several points of view. This in itself greatly increases understanding of the action as a whole.

The use of action-replay is based on an extended version of '5W–H' (outlined in the chapter on *Assessment*). Having decided on a title for the incident, group members can then answer the questions of who, when, where, what, why, and how.

Thinking for example of *who* was involved might involve analysing the characters in some depth. What were they like in age and appearance, and what were their relations to the person re-creating the incident? More important, what was going on in their heads? What was their mood, their intention, and their state of mind? By thinking about each of the participants in this way, a lot can be revealed about the mechanics underlying the incident as a whole.

Next the questions as to *when* and *where* need to be answered. It is less important to know the Greenwich Mean Time and the Ordnance Survey grid reference than to have the personal connotations of time and place: 'in John's house', 'three weeks after I started my last job', or 'not long after we'd met'. This information too can pinpoint the underlying reasons for events.

The kernel of the analysis then follows: *what* happened? This might involve a description of events from one or more points of view, or the writing of a script, followed by a role-play of the events themselves.

For example, a man might role-play a scene in a pub in which he is challenged to a fight. He has a reputation for violence which he wishes to put behind him; but numerous youngsters trying to make their name want to prove themselves against him. The role-play might depict such an approach, the ensuing affray (without actual blows), and perhaps subsequent arrest.

Such a role-play, and its playback if recorded on video, can then be used as material for tackling the question *why* and *how*. Why did this incident take place? How could it have been dealt with differently? Are there other means of handling such an incident which would have had a better outcome for the individuals involved? For most incidents there are many alternative courses of action. In the case of our man in the bar, for example, instead of fighting, what else could he have done?

Walked away?

Offered his challenger a drink?

Explained the problem to him?

Asked a friend to intervene?

Ignored him?

Arranged to meet him elsewhere?

Diverted the challenge in some way?

Told him he was ill?

Told him the police were watching him?

Gone to the pub with his wife?

Gone to the pub accompanied by a large Alsatian?

The consequences of each of these alternative reactions could then be worked out, using modelling or role-playing if necessary. The analysis should have helped to pinpoint exactly where changes could have been made, and what would have been their likely outcomes.

Used in this way, critical incidents analysis is really a combination of methods rather than a single method on its own; its distinctive contribution is the careful dissection of character and plot which, coupled with role-playing, can serve to re-create incidents as close to the reality as possible. A session, or series of sessions, looking at incidents in this way, can be very productive in focussing attention on problems and how to deal with them in a more general sense.

The intensive analysis of social skills problems, using some of the above methods, can be a very demanding process, and it is essential not to lose sight of other aspects of social situations which influence events in significant ways. One kind of learning, which helps to add spice to an understanding of interaction, is the direct experience of some of the distortions that can take place in even the simplest sorts of communication. No formal lecture or printed page could match the effectiveness of Whispers – an easily organized group exercise – in bringing home the risks we all take when we utter the merest word. Whispers is described in the box below.

Another form of 'learning by doing' which, though rudimentary, has enormous

---

Whispers

Whispers is a particularly intriguing way of looking at the process of social communication, and in particular the growth of distortions of the kind that give rise to rumours. The prototype of the game is Bartlett's study of how something changes when it is recalled by a group of people in a series. By showing one individual a drawing, then asking him to sketch it from memory, showing this sketch to a second person who is asked to sketch *it* from memory, and so on, he discovered some of the kinds of distortion that take place when we pass on imperfect information in this way. This can also be done with stories, often with great impact. One individual is asked to read a story (for example from the newspaper) to another, who then retails his remembrance of it to a third, and so on. Over the course of ten people or so the story can be completely forgotten, absurdly simplified, or even turned into another story completely divergent from the first. For even greater impact, video can be used: the passing over of the story from one individual to another can be recorded, or the story as told by each group member can be recorded as a news item and the whole series then played back in turn. If you have no video, an audio-tape will do. The resultant amusement is paralleled in value only by the recognition that emerges of the rumour-building pro-cess in action. It is worthwhile reflecting, if you have used a newspaper item, on how much distortion might have been there even before you started.

This exercise produces very valuable discussion: of the kinds of change that take place; of the variety of situations in which this distortion can occur; and on possible ways of recognizing when information has been distorted.

value in promoting social skill, is the *self-presentation* exercise. This can take a number of forms, all of which involve the common element of asking individuals to put themselves across directly to others – usually by giving a short talk on a subject of their own choosing.

One such exercise – 'My ten best points' – is described on page 100; it violates deeply entrenched taboos of modesty and may even be impossible for some people. Others, however, find it deeply engaging and productive; they may never have thought of themselves in that way before. Such a point applies, in some respects, to the whole gamut of social skills training methods. Individuals can become more competent socially, can change unrecognizably in dramatically short periods, can overcome inhibitions, acquire subtlety, and make startling gains in confidence – all of these can be accomplished, if the opportunities are simply made available.

The kinds of skill discussed in this section – of handling social interaction in settings as diverse as the home, pub, or courtroom – are obviously basic to satisfactory functioning in the world most of us inhabit today. In the next section we turn to a related, but in some ways more fundamental, set of skills: those associated with the solving of problems and the translation of thinking into action. While to many the notion of importing a 'method' into the subtle world of personal problems may seem alien, a brief glance at the kinds of skill involved – of getting information and deciding how to use it, for example – when contrasted with the number of problems that derive from a *lack* of these skills, should convince the sceptic of the advantages of approaching them in some basically systematic manner.

2 *Exercises in problem solving and related skills*: Though most of us are capable of solving a large number of minor problems on an everyday basis, we rarely see these as having much in common with the problems confronted by science or technology on a massive scale. Yet in some way there must be a link, for the latter, in a slow and stumbling evolution of steps and stages, developed out of the former. In so doing, science and technology transformed the problem-solving process – indeed, they did so with such thoroughness that today it seems inaccessible to most people. Seldom have the results of these efforts been directed back at the kinds of problem individuals face in the course of living their lives. In more recent years, however, systematic approaches to solving human problems have been not only advocated but also applied with great effect, in industrial management and the running of large organizations. Most of us probably experience the results as being all too similar to the approach of the sciences, suitably cleansed of human content; and it is unlikely that any single problem-solving system could be applied to the personal area just as it stands. The central idea, however – of approaching problem solving in some structured way, and tackling it through a set of clearly defined stages – seems at bottom to be a sound one, and provides one of the cornerstones of this book.

A self-presentation exercise: 'My ten best points'
We have already come across the use of self-presentation exercises in assessment, but there are other uses to which these can be put, which involve learning to a considerable extent. A self-presentation exercise is obviously more productive for both assessment and learning purposes if individuals are asked to give a talk about themselves. To make this easier (or, some claim, more difficult), the task can be structured by asking people to give a talk entitled, for example, 'My ten best points'. Alternatively, you can ask individuals to write best points associated with the letters of their first name (or second, or both), like this:

Considerate
Honest
Rebellious
Interesting
Sexy.

In either case, group members are asked to think about (and write down if necessary) what they see as their best points, and to give a talk (either to the group or on video) about them, lasting not more than two minutes (though often, in fact, one minute is better).

In appraising the performance, individuals can use a variety of self-presentation scales, person-perception scales like those described in the assessment chapter, or scales constructed specially for the purpose. Discussion can then focus on the different aspects of the performance, on the various points mentioned, on the variety of approaches used (and these will vary from sermons, to intimate *tête a têtes*, to songs), and on the relationship between good and bad points.

Most people, initially diffident, find this an exhilarating learning experience – particularly if they are accustomed, as many people are, to thinking of themselves in terms of bad points; much of the exercise's value stems simply from the positive boost it gives to those who take part in it.

What is the nature of problem-solving systems? In essence they are simply formulae that guide us into activities – *things to do* that will make solutions to problems more readily available. Unlike computer programmes, they cannot guarantee answers: they do not lead us by a series of logical steps to conclusions that are unique and inviolable. For the most part they produce ideas in quantity, from which a solution can be chosen; and the use of them does not demand a high I.Q. or a sophisticated understanding of any kind of theory. Successful problem solving may, however, require some kinds of skill; and it is these, and the business of acquiring them, that the present section seeks to describe.

Problem-solving systems

Problem-solving systems range widely in form and complexity, from the humble '5W–H', which helps us to generate ideas on some topic, to the scientific method itself, which designates rules and working procedures in many fields of inquiry and is one of the centrepieces of Western culture. The application of problem solving might involve us in anything from counting to ten, sitting down, and thinking before acting, to making a series of decisions in a team, or to carrying out experiments under carefully controlled conditions. Within such variation, we can, however, detect a number of common elements:

1 *an information-gathering stage*: defining and describing the problem to be solved in as much detail as possible;
2 *generating alternative solutions*: putting together as many ways as possible of solving the problem in question;
3 *formulating a plan of action* based on trying out in practice one or more of the possible solutions;
4 *checking the results* to see if the problem has been solved; and, if not, why not.

All of these elements, like the social skills of the last section, consist of activities that have to be *learned*. There is no magic process by which we come to manage our money, handle conflicts, or make complex decisions, without sometimes watching others, taking advice, making our own mistakes, and storing up a bank of experience for ourselves. The job could, however, be made easier for many people by the use of exercises specifically designed to help develop such skills; particularly so for individuals beset with problems in these areas, who feel motivated to do something about them. We can look at some examples of such exercises related to different phases of the problem-solving process, for the most essential skills including:

information search
decision making
problem solving as a whole.

Information search

Information is a vital ingredient in problem solving. Though it can hardly solve a problem by itself, it can widen and deepen the quality of decision making that precedes successful action. Sometimes all the information required is lying ready to hand, in the minds of participants in the problem-solving process, or is easily accessible from a nearby source.

A lot of information is, however, less freely available. It has to be tracked down, sniffed out, and painstakingly put together in a form that makes it useful for the immediate task of solving personal problems. Some individuals have a natural talent for this; others may never even have thought that it sometimes makes sense to delay action until more is known about a problem. Even if those in the latter group wanted to, they might not have been able to find the necessary information for lack of the necessary skills.

The skills of finding information are keys to survival in the present day – for finding out about jobs or places to live; about the law in its slow expansion into every sphere of our lives; about the management of money (regardless of how much or how little we have); and about anything else we may want to do, from buying vegetables to going on a holiday abroad. These skills can be developed by exercises designed to illustrate, and allow for practice in, the business of acquiring information on a given topic. Some ways of doing this might include:

1 the use of case studies which illustrate the information-getting process;
2 asking group members, in group discussion, to pool their experience of collecting information on some topic, and describing the sources they have personally found useful;
3 during counselling sessions, working through particular problems and pointing out specific places from which information can be obtained;
4 the setting of information-finding *projects*. Individuals – working alone or in a group – are asked to gather as much information as possible on some limited topic, such as places to find accommodation, the cheapest places to shop, or even sources of information of some particular kind. If such projects are written up they can then be used by subsequent generations of problem solvers; an additional related exercise might be the presentation of project results to the group as a whole.

Below is an account of another information-search exercise which can easily be organized with a small group.

Decision making
Decision making is a large and complex area of human behaviour, and most investigation of it has concentrated on decisions in the upper reaches of business management, social policy formation, or international relations. An as-yet-unmet need exists for similar work on decision making in everyday life, as practised by ordinary individuals beset with their own personal problems. Meanwhile, however, some headway can be made by adapting techniques developed for management training to more mundane topics than investment decisions or the planning of a deep space probe. We can look briefly here at some ways of approaching this area.

An information-search exercise

In its simplest form this exercise would consist of giving to an individual or group a list of facts or points on some topic, e.g. a list of things to look for when renting a flat, or buying a car. Another member of the group is then invited to interview the first, and to try to find out as many as possible of the points of information made available to the first. This not only imparts the information, but also gives practice in asking the most relevant kinds of question.

The exercise can be elaborated in two ways. First, the information, rather than being presented ready-made, has to be generated by an individual or group. Another individual or group has to generate a set of questions designed to elicit that information. The similarities and differences in the two lists of points generated (which would have to be limited to, say, ten items) can provide substance for later discussion. Some topics which might be dealt with in this way include:

getting a job	setting up a small business
buying a car	moving to a new area
having home repairs done	coping with debts of some kind.

Individuals or groups can be given scores for the task, according to how many 'right' questions they ask as against how many of little information-producing value.

A second level can be added to this exercise by installing observers who look in on the information-finding interviews and rate those asking the questions on some pre-arranged scales, e.g. of confidence, clarity of questions, persistence, logic, economy, or politeness. This also provides key points for discussion afterwards.

All of these aspects could be combined in an exercise in which interviewer and interviewee are briefed on the complementary aspects of one problem, e.g. one is a car buyer who has to ask key questions about a car; the other is a car salesman who asks key questions about the buyer's credit-worthiness. Each initially has to generate *answers* to questions he anticipates the *other* person should ask. He can then assign a score to the other person's information-getting skills, and an observer can rate both of them on their performance as interviewers.

Case histories are an invaluable resource in this respect. A simple outline of a decision made by someone with a particular problem, with some information about how they arrived at it, can provoke pointed discussion on the same problem as experienced by others. Such a case history might consist of a character sketch and some background details as in the example given below.

The history of a decision
John is 35 years old, a scaffolder, earning £90 per week net, separated from his wife and paying £45 per week as a voluntary contribution to her maintenance and that of their three children. Two of the children are under school age and his wife cannot go out to work. He is living with a woman who is shortly expecting a child; they occupy a rented flat which costs £17 per week and they are finding things difficult financially. His wife asks him for additional help to meet fuel bills during a period of cold weather, and for new school clothes for the eldest child. John is not sure what to do.

This sketch can serve as a hand-out which is given to individuals working alone or in small groups. They have simply to decide what John should do in these circumstances. One member of a 'team' (if you are working in teams) should keep a record of the discussion and the directions it took, including any blind alleys. Any alternatives to the main choice of action should also be decided upon. The whole process could then be presented to a larger group, or compared with decisions made by other 'teams' working on the same problem.

Sentencing exercises are slightly more organized forms of case history. Case notes are provided on offenders who are to appear in court, and small 'benches' of group members deliberate and then decide on the sentences they would award in each case. Alternatively, other group members can themselves write the case notes. Again maximum benefit is derived if the whole process is followed by discussion of the pros and cons involved in each decision.

This exercise can be made more formal still in order to reveal the 'fine grain' of the decision-making process. What information do individuals use in making decisions? By breaking down information into single items, it is possible to look at how some kinds of decision are made. Each item of information about a case – for example, age, marital status, occupation, job history, health, previous convictions, and many more – can be typed on a separate sheet. The sheets are then inserted in a folder in such a way that only the title of the sheet is visible – e.g. *Information on Job History, Family Background* – and participants in the exercise are asked to make a decision about sentencing after searching through the information in whatever order they choose. They can then stop scrutinizing the information at whatever point they feel happy about making a decision. By recording the order in which items were consulted, the number of them consulted, and the ways in which different individuals use the information, it is possible to gain a great deal of insight into the fabric of decision making and the numerous factors that have an effect upon it.

Identifying assumptions is a central component of gaining further insight into the making of decisions. A discussion around decision making can be structured in such a way as to focus attention on assumptions by feeding in questions on general issues applicable to specific decisions. For example, was the decision to assault a particular policeman the result of that policeman's behaviour, or of beliefs about the police held by the attacker? What was the importance of each? Many other items like this are susceptible to similar analysis. At a more basic level, assumptions can be examined by presenting individuals with a photograph or sketch depicting, for example, someone's living room. Questions are then asked about the content of the sketch, which elicit hidden assumptions made on looking at it: there are certain conclusions that can be drawn from the picture, e.g. that there is a lamp on top of the television; but there are others that cannot, e.g. that the man and woman in the picture are husband and wife. Pictures and questions on many topics could be put together for this purpose.

Personal decisions can be looked at in a number of ways. If one individual in a group is happy to do so, he could be invited to describe to the rest of the group how he arrived at a particular decision; discussion could focus not only on the circumstances of that particular decision, but also more generally on the kinds of factor to be taken into account in making a decision of that kind. A useful technique for breaking down such decisions is known as 'force field analysis'. This is essentially an application of brainstorming methods to the business of decision making. All we do is generate lists of ideas for and against any course of action: its pros and cons, advantages and disadvantages. We have to imagine that around any decision, plan, or pattern of action, there is a

Force field analysis of a marriage crisis

Things that keep us together   Things that drive us apart

Things we need to change to solve this marriage crisis:

'field of force' whose tensions have to be resolved – just as the movement of a ball on an inclined plane, to use a mechanical analogy – is a product of the forces acting on it. This might be applied to several distinct courses of action to see which one emerges as most favourable, as having the most advantages; or it might be applied to some background pattern of action round a decision, for example, to change spending habits, cut down on smoking, or help to resolve a crisis in a marriage as illustrated in the accompanying force field table adapted from the Saskatchewan Newstart (1973) *Life Skills Coaching Manual*.

Problem solving

The problem-solving process itself can be used to construct a system of exercises for groups that are interested in developing problem-solving skills. There are a number of contributory factors involved in this: individuals need to see that a problem-solving 'system' works, by having its use illustrated in relation to a familiar problem; they need to have the approach presented in a way in which it can be readily understood and applied; and they need to use it themselves, to gain direct experience of its working – as with other skills, the best way to improve this is by trying it in practice.

Problem-solving skills can be improved by presenting to a group a way of coping with problems, and demonstrating its value in action. It might then be necessary to deal with different aspects of the skill (information search, generating ideas, decision making) separately, before trying to apply the whole approach to the solution of some particular problem. Though lengthy, this can pay off in concrete – and enduring – results.

3 *Simulations*: These are amongst the most elaborate, yet in many ways the most absorbing, of learning methods that can be used in the *doing* area. In one sense they are based on the assumption that the best method of learning is by experiencing something directly oneself: if this is not possible, for whatever reason, then the next best thing is to simulate it. Simulations are structured sets of activities, with assigned roles, depicting actual events or situations, which can be used by groups to give their members experience in the kinds of question and problem that can arise in that situation in real life. They can range in scale and verisimilitude from relatively simple game-like tasks lasting half an hour, to complex re-creations of actual historical incidents lasting several days, and may vary greatly in structure, depending on the number of rules in operation – which in turn depends on what is being simulated.

Thus we can have simulated news broadcasts, court hearings, or moon landings, diplomatic wrangles, or all-out wars. In fact, anything at all that happens with some degree of order in real life can be simulated: the job interview with its predetermined roles and sets of expectations; the courtroom, tribunal, or public inquiry with established patterns of procedure; the market-place, or any other meeting point between groups or individuals with complementary (or rival) kinds of aims and intentions. Dimensions, too, are no problem: the job in question can be plumber or Prime Minister, the market-place a butcher's shop or the whole economic system of a country. The only common requirement is that some of the elements of the 'real' world be present in the simulation.

The purpose of a simulation is to afford opportunities for the development of skills appropriate to the event or area of life being simulated. In practice, simulations incorporate many of the methods of social skills training – role-playing, self-presentation, critical incident 'replays' – *and* many key features of problem solving, information search, and decision making. But, in addition, they also frequently involve exchange of actual information on the areas they portray, and touch closely on many topics with an attitudinal or 'feeling' component. Their overarching flexibility means they can be stretched in almost any direction to suit the purposes of the user.

In spite of their potential sophistication, therefore, simulations can be used for the most mundane of day-to-day events, and still have some pay-off in learning. Any problem that exists can be simulated by a group. You can easily make up simulations of your own representing some situation familiar to you. The box below describes just one ordinary setting that can be simulated with some unexpected effects.

A simulation: Tenement
Tenement is a simulation developed and marketed by Shelter. It combines elements of role-play and problem solving with a substantial informational content.

Tenement portrays a multi-occupied house, its grasping landlord, and six sets of occupants, ranging from an old-age pensioner who lives alone to a married couple with four children. At their disposal are six helping agencies, such as the Department of Employment, Citizens Advice Bureau, and a Rent Tribunal. Briefings are provided for each of the participants; a minimum of thirteen players is required, with a likely maximum of twenty-five, if individual parts are shared. Playing time can vary from forty minutes to one-and-a-half hours, during which the occupants of the house have to try to better their accommodation problems by using any or all of the agencies that are available.

Though some of the information needs constant revision, and the role of the Social Services Department has for some reason been omitted, these problems can easily be rectified. The simulation can be enhanced by recording some of the action on video-tape, and playing it back for discussion at the end. The notes provide discussion points for an overall review.

Using learning procedures in practice

The survey of methods which forms the bulk of this chapter is now complete. In this section, we would like to look briefly at some illustrations of how the methods might be used in practice, before concluding with a summary table which forms part of the curriculum matrix.

In this section, we can begin by taking an example of a typical problem from each of the areas *knowing*, *feeling*, and *doing*, before going on to give an example that would involve all three. We should say, first, that these examples are inevitably very cursory in the methods they suggest (and in the specimen problems they set) and, second, that the suggestions are in no sense the 'correct' ones: users of the approach will have to judge the needs of individual cases in their own right. The suggestions are *purely illustrative*.

KNOWING

One of the most frequently encountered problems in the area of information deficits which users of this approach might come across lies in the area of job search. Individuals or groups who have used the method in action have produced many problems in this area, e.g. not knowing their own skills; how to go about looking for a job, how to get one, or how to keep one; their rights in employment; and many others besides. Some of the kinds of information we could give them, and methods we could use to do so, might include:

- a lecture or talk on a given kind of job
- a visit to a factory or place of work
- a programmed package on some basic knowledge of a job
- a demonstration of how to write a letter of application
- information leaflets on training opportunities
- information on the laws protecting them in their work
- a differential aptitude test measuring some of their skills
- a survey of the jobs they have done aimed at eliciting 'hidden' skills.

Though, of course, individual needs will vary, it is not unlikely that most groups will contain some members who lack some, if not most, of the information that the above methods could generate. These are only some superficial examples; there are thousands more.

FEELING

In this area we can use a different example which certainly involves emotional if not attitudinal problems for most people: the problem of violence. The kinds of problem individuals name in this area vary enormously, from lack of self-control or spontaneous outbursts of violence to quite coherently worked out sets of prejudices or beliefs. Some of the methods we might use to look at and change the feelings and attitudes involved are:

- peer interviews between violence-prone individuals
- role-plays of violent incidents
- counselling by individuals or groups
- a fishbowl-group discussion of attitudes towards minority groups
- pattern notes on, e.g., 'lost temper'
- group self-ratings and mutual ratings on some aspects of violence
- 'trust' exercises in groups for whom this is a problem.

Again, in the area of violence, it would be, in our view, extremely unlikely if there were not individuals who could learn or change something about themselves as a result of some of these exercises pitched even at the most general level. With knowledge of individual needs the exercises can be made even more specific and effective.

DOING

An example of a social or life skill area with which many individuals and groups have problems is that of finding information from an unwilling source. Most people encounter this problem sooner or later; reactions to it may vary from giving up altogether to bringing more problems on oneself by causing trouble and embarrassment. Some things we could try in this area might include:

- breakdown of the skill into important parts
- using slides of facial expressions to test accuracy of perception
- graded information-search exercises for groups
- modelling of critical incidents by competent individuals
- video feedback of performance in 'fact-finding' role-plays
- simulations which involve the obtaining and use of information
- survey project carried out by group members
- actual information search in a specific relevant area.

Once again it is unlikely that individuals who express problems in this area could not benefit to some extent from these exercises; even the increase in confidence that results from finding some critical information would produce positive effects. But the application of some of these methods to specifically identified problem areas, and their use in a series, would probably train individuals to be better at finding the information they need. And again, acquaintance with a specific group would enable users to tailor the chosen methods to the specific needs of the group.

A COMPOSITE PROBLEM AREA

It is more common, of course, to find that the problems individuals and groups identify during the use of this method involve desired changes in all three of the areas of *knowing*, *feeling*, and *doing*. Apart from the ubiquitous problem of overlap – of deciding to which area many problems belong in the first place – the business of surviving in society throws up problems often requiring changes at all three 'levels' simultaneously. The example we might use here is that of making complaints, a process sufficiently difficult to be off-putting to most people, and all too often mishandled by those who have fewer inhibitions about it. To become effective at complaining requires some of the items described in the accompanying table.

What we need is . . .	*To do with . . .*	*Obtainable by . . .*
Some INFORMATION	The appropriate person to whom complaint should be made. Our rights in the situation in question. The exact nature of the complaint.	Reading leaflets from, e.g., the Office of Fair Trading, or *How to Complain* by Christopher Ward. Talk by a solicitor. Peer interviews.
Some ATTITUDES and FEELINGS	Having the necessary confidence. Believing that, if the case is valid, we will get satisfaction.	Counselling sessions. Role-plays of critical incidents. Group discussion.
Some SKILLS	Having self-control if provoked. Being firm in the face of possible hostility. Communicating our intentions clearly.	Role-play and rehearsal of complaint. Video self-presentation exercise. Group ratings of 'complaining' skill.

So, for the problems individuals might experience in this area, some learning may be required at all three of these levels: experience suggests this is more than likely. For any actual case of complaining, we could complete the right-hand column of the table in a highly specific manner and so end up with a set of plans for taking action on the particular issue at stake.

The majority of the problems that individuals have are of this kind. Examples could be multiplied, but we leave it to users of the manual to conjure up some of their own, or simply to ask some appropriate group with whom they are working, and to imagine some methods that could be used with the problems so produced.

These suggested methods – those surveyed in this chapter and suggested above for use in specific problem areas – are the elements, when we get used to this approach in action, of *programmes*. Programmes, which are the subject of a later chapter, are the results of experience with given problems; they are those methods that, when used together with a given group in a given area of difficulty, have been found to pay off in results. But they are composed in each case of some of the methods and materials we have gone through under the headings of *Knowing*, *Feeling*, and *Doing* in the preceding pages.

Most problems are 'composite' in the sense that complaining is: they need tackling by engendering change on several levels at once. Programmes permit changes to occur in as many ways as possible by including methods and materials drawn from every relevant area of learning which individuals might identify. To give an overall, encapsulated picture of the diversity of these areas, the summary table below outlines the contents of the survey this chapter has undertaken. This in its turn is just one section of the matrix presented at the beginning of this book.

Learning procedures: section of the curriculum matrix

	Knowing	*Feeling*	*Doing*
Learning procedures	Direct teaching methods	Counselling methods	Social skills training methods
	Self-organized learning	Group discussion	Problem solving and related methods
	Vocational guidance materials	Role-play	Simulations
	Brainstorming methods	Groupwork methods	
	Group discussion		

Note: See page 139 for the completed curriculum matrix.

Notes and references

LEARNING RESOURCES IN GENERAL

Two useful general books on learning resources and direct teaching are: L. C. Taylor (1972) *Resources for Learning* (Harmondsworth: Penguin); and P. MacMillan and L. Powell (1973) *An Induction Course for Teaching in Education and Industry* (London: Pitman Publishing).

For information and materials in the audiovisual aids area, the most useful sources of help are: National Audio-Visual Aids Centre, 254–56 Belsize Road, London NW6; and National Committee for Audio-Visual Aids in Education at the same address. These organizations can provide information, equipment, training, films, and many other resources, and publish periodicals on educational aids.

ON INDIVIDUALIZED LEARNING

For a discussion of programmed learning, see Taylor (1972) mentioned above, and also: E. Fry (1963) *Teaching Machines and Programmed Instruction* (New York: McGraw-Hill); and A. Howe and A. J. Romiszowski (annual) *APLET Yearbook of Educational and Instructional Technology* (London: Kogan Page).

A wide range of programmed texts and other self-instruction aids can be obtained from Educational Services Ltd. These are aimed predominantly at practical skills and the information associated with them, e.g. *H.G.V. Driver's Manual: A Guide to the Driving Test*; and they are available from Educational Services Ltd., St. Lawrence House, 29–31 Broad Street, Bristol BS1 2HF. E.S.L. are also suppliers of *Gateway*, a series of audio-tape and filmstrip presentations for self-instruction in some practical skills and topics of general educational interest.

On the construction of self-organized learning packages, see: R. B. Johnson and S. R. Johnson (1975) *Towards Individualized Learning: Developer's Guide to Self-instruction* (London: Addison-Wesley); and J. A. Jeanneau (1973) *Small Business Management: Instructor's Manual* (Vols. 1–5) (Prince Albert, Saskatchewan: Training, Research and Development Section, Department of Manpower and Immigration).

For remedial literacy teaching, the most useful course of action is to contact local colleges or teachers engaged in running courses in this area. Some valuable background and suggestions for resources are given in C. Longley (ed.) (1975) *Adult Literacy Handbook* (London: BBC Publications). Of particular value in this field is the Dico 'type-to-read' system, which can be used as a self-instruction package both for typing *and* learning to read: R. G. Flanders (1976) *Type to Read with the New Dico System* (London: Dico Educational International).

For an account of learning exchanges and how they work, see once again the book by Taylor (1972) mentioned above, and also: I. Illich (1970) *Deschooling Society* (Harmondsworth: Penguin); and J. Holt (1976) *Instead of Education* (Harmondsworth: Penguin).

MATERIALS USED IN VOCATIONAL GUIDANCE

A number of different sets of materials, and guides to jobs and careers, are currently available. They include: *Signposts*, which you should be able to find in the Careers Service of the Local Education Authority – ask the Careers Officer for help; *Speedcop*, a careers game prepared by B. Hopson, available from the Hobson Press, Bateman Street, Cambridge; and *CODOT, Classification of Occupations and Directory of Occupational*

Titles, a cross-indexed guide to occupations, published by HMSO, 49 High Holborn, London WC1V 6HB. In addition, many useful ideas in the area of vocational guidance can be found in: B. Hopson and P. Hough (1973) *Exercises in Personal and Career Development* (Cambridge: Careers Research and Advisory Centre), which is itself a supplier of valuable materials and information on many aspects of vocational guidance.

ON BRAINSTORMING METHODS

An outline of brainstorming and its uses in learning and problem solving can be found in K. Jackson (1975) *The Art of Solving Problems* (London: Heinemann) – also published by English Universities Press as part of the *Teach Yourself* series. See also P. R. Whitfield (1975) *Creativity in Industry* (Harmondsworth: Penguin).

For more about pattern notes, see T. Buzan (1974) *Use Your Head* (London: BBC Publications).

GROUP DISCUSSION

An indispensable introduction to the use of group discussion and its value as a learning method is M. L. J. Abercrombie (1969) *The Anatomy of Judgement* (Harmondsworth: Penguin). For a fuller treatment, see also her (1974) *Aims and Techniques of Group Teaching* (London: Society for Research in Higher Education).

COUNSELLING AND RELATED METHODS

An introduction to counselling is given by J. Shaw (1973) *Basic Counselling* (Stockport, Cheshire: Vernon Scott Associates). Other useful sources include: C. Rogers (1965) *Client Centred Therapy* (London: Constable); and B. Mackinnon and N. Falsenfield (1971) *Group Counselling and Psychotherapy with Adolescents* (New York: Columbia University Press).

A recent book which includes discussion of specific techniques is J. Adams, J. Hayes, and B. Hopson (1977) *Transition: Understanding and Managing Personal Change* (London: Martin Robertson). See also A. G. Watts (ed.) (1977) *Counselling at Work*, a collection of papers on different aspects of counselling, published by the recently instituted British Association for Counselling, from whom further information and advice can be obtained. You can contact them at the National Council of Social Service, 26 Bedford Square, London WC1B 3HU.

ON ROLE-PLAYING

For an introduction to role-playing methods, see J. V. Flowers (1975) Simulation and

Roleplaying Methods, in, F. H. Kanfer and A. P. Goldstein *Helping People Change: A Textbook of Methods* (Oxford: Pergamon). The role-playing 'experiment' mentioned here was carried out by the American psychologist P. Zimbardo and others, and is described more fully in P. Zimbardo *et al.* (1973) The Mind is a Formidable Jailer – A Pirandellian Prison, in, *The New York Times*, 8 April.

GROUPWORK AND RELATED METHODS

Many books have been written on groupwork and on the various 'schools' of thought within it. Possibly the most useful all-round introduction is T. Douglas (1976) *Group-work Practice* (London: Tavistock). Some other general books on the range of methods that are available are: L. Button (1974) *Developmental Group Work with Adolescents* (London: University of London Press); F. H. Kanfer and A. P. Goldstein (1975) *Helping People Change: A Textbook of Methods* (Oxford: Pergamon); and S. D. Rose (1977) *Group Therapy – A Behavioural Approach* (Hemel Hempstead, Hertfordshire: Prentice-Hall).

For more details on some of the specialized ways of working, see the following:

– on Encounter Groups: C. Rogers (1973) *Encounter Groups* (Harmondsworth: Penguin); and W. C. Schutz (1973) *Joy* (Harmondsworth: Penguin);
– on T-groups: A. Blumberg and R. T. Golembiewski (1976) *Learning and Change in Groups* (Harmondsworth: Penguin);
– on Gestalt Therapy: F. Perls, R. Hefferline, and P. Goodman (1973) *Gestalt Therapy* (Harmondsworth: Penguin);
– on Transactional Analysis: E. Berne (1970) *Games People Play* (Harmondsworth: Penguin); T. Harris (1973) *I'm O.K., You're O.K.* (London: Cape);
– on Growth Games: H. R. Lewis and H. S. Streitfeld (1970) *Growth Games* (London: Souvenir Press); and J. W. Pfieffer and J. E. Jones (1970) *A Handbook of Structured Experiences for Human Relations Training* (Iowa City, Iowa: University Associates Press).

SOCIAL SKILLS TRAINING METHODS

Though much has been written about social skills training, the actual amount of material available for running your own training exercises is rather small. The best possible course of action is to design your own: think about the skills in which you are interested, and assemble some basic exercises which seemingly might help individuals acquire them – and then try them out.

For help in putting such an exercise together, the most useful sources we have found are the *Life Skills Coaching Manual* (1973) and the *Socanic Coaching Manual* (1972) produced by the Saskatchewan Newstart project, under the auspices of the Department of Manpower and Immigration, Prince Albert, Saskatchewan. These, together with some additional training manuals for use with specific groups (for example, adolescents and offenders) and a collection of papers on life skills, were available from: Information Canada, Publications Satellite, P.O. Box 1565, Prince Albert, Saskatchewan S6V 5T2, Canada. Though the *Life Skills Coaching Manual* is at present out of print, further editions may be forthcoming, or you may be able to obtain it from libraries or training colleges in Britain.

These manuals cover a wide range of skills, from face-to-face communicative skills to those involved in making complex decisions. For ideas and suggestions on some basic social skills, see the following: M. Argyle (1973) *Social Interaction* (London: Tavistock) – Chapter 10 outlines some of the previous work on social skills training; P. Trower, B. Bryant, and M. Argyle (1978) *Social Skills and Mental Health* (London: Methuen) – a review of work on basic social skills training, incorporating a training manual for these skills; I. Falloon, P. Lindley, and R. McDonald (1974) *Social Training: A Manual* (London: Psychological Treatment Section, Maudsley Hospital), which outlines a ten-session course for developing basic social skills; and N. Rackham and T. Morgan (1977) *Behaviour Analysis in Training* (Maidenhead, Berkshire: McGraw-Hill), which looks at methods of training social skills used in industry. See also P. G. Zimbardo (1977) *Shyness* (Reading, Massachusetts: Addison-Wesley).

The 'basic social skills' exercises outlined here are derived from ideas in M. Argyle (1975) *Bodily Communication* (London: Methuen); I. Falloon, P. Lindley, and R. McDonald (1974) as above; and S. M. Jourard (1963) An Exploratory Study of Body-Accessibility, in, *British Journal of Social and Clinical Psychology* 5: 221–31.

The use of modelling as a training method is based on the work of the 'social learning' theorists, which is described in full by A. Bandura (1970) *Principles of Behaviour Modification* (London: Holt, Rhinehart and Winston). Modelling has been used successfully in social skills training with several groups, notably juvenile offenders. See I. Sarason (1968) Verbal Learning, Modelling, and Juvenile Delinquency, in *American Psychologist* 23: 254–66; and I. Sarason and V. J. Ganzer (1973) Modelling and Group Discussion in the Rehabilitation of Juvenile Delinquents, in, *Journal of Counselling Psychology* 20: 442–49. The 'using-the-telephone' and 'self-presentation' exercises described here have been modified from material available in the *Life Skills Coaching Manual* (1973), mentioned above. *Whispers* is an extension of an experiment carried out by F. C. Bartlett, and described in his *Remembering* (1932; Cambridge: Cambridge University Press).

INFORMATION-SEARCH EXERCISES

The organization of any information-search exercise depends on the kind of information involved, and the uses to which it will be put; again it is probably best if you can design your own, suited to the needs of some particular group. Some ideas on the development of information-finding skills are contained in: T. Buzan (1974) *Use Your Head* (London: BBC Publications); and Saskatchewan Newstart (1973) *Life Skills Coaching Manual* and (1972) *Socanic Coaching Manual* (Prince Albert, Saskatchewan: Department of Manpower and Immigration).

Some ideas for information-finding projects which could be adapted to suit many purposes can be found in J. Rennie, E. A. Lunzer, and W. T. Williams (1974) *Social Education: An Experiment in Four Secondary Schools*, Schools Council Working Paper 51 (London: Evans/Methuen Educational).

DECISION-MAKING EXERCISES

Once again, many decision-making exercises of the kind described here can be invented for the purposes of particular individuals and groups. For some other illustrations of the use of such exercises, see: P. McPhail (1972) *In Other People's Shoes* (Harlow: Longman); Saskatchewan Newstart (1973) as above; L. T. Wilkins (1967) *Social Policy, Action, and Research* (London: Tavistock), for a 'sentencing' exercise; and C. Adams, S. Gagg, and G. Tayar (1973, 1974) *Living Decisions in Family and Community* (Vols. 1 and 2) (London: BBC Publications).

ON PROBLEM SOLVING

As suggested in the text, a full-scale problem-solving exercise would probably have to be an amalgam of different types of other exercise, incorporating as it does the skills of finding information, generating ideas, making decisions, and putting them into effect. However, many additional ideas and pointers towards other fertile areas can be obtained from the following: E. de Bono (1971) *The Use of Lateral Thinking* (Harmondsworth: Penguin), (1976) *Teaching Thinking* (London: Maurice Temple Smith), or any of his other many books; T. Buzan (1974) *Use Your Head* (London: BBC Publications); K. Jackson (1975) *The Art of Solving Problems* (London: Heinemann), and in the *Teach Yourself* series of books published by English Universities Press; and G. Spivack, J. J. Platt, and M. B. Shure (1976) *The Problem-Solving Approach to Adjustment* (San Francisco: Jossey-Bass). The approach of this last book is in many ways closer to that of the present volume than any other we have come across.

E. de Bono's books, plus a great range of material for use in the teaching of problem solving, are available from Direct Education Services, 1 Alfred St., Blandford Forum, Dorset, who can furnish a catalogue of the resources they provide.

SIMULATIONS

The nature of simulations and their use, together with descriptions of many specific games and simulation exercises, are covered in the following: G. I. Gibbs (ed.) (1974) *Handbook of Games and Simulation Exercises* (London: E. and F. N. Spon); M. Inbar and C. S. Stoll (1972) *Simulation and Gaming in Social Science* (New York: The Free Press); and J. Taylor and R. Walford (1972) *Simulation in the Classroom* (Harmondsworth: Penguin).

The *Tenement* simulation described in the text is available in shorter and longer forms from: Shelter, National Campaign for the Homeless, Community Education Programme, 157 Waterloo Road, London SE1 8UU.

An especially useful series of nine simulations graded in order of complexity can be obtained from the Inner London Education Authority, Learning Materials Service, Publishing Centre, Highbury Station Road, London N1 1SB. Their catalogue describes these and many other materials which they can supply.

COMPLAINING

A highly readable handbook on some of the vagaries of making complaints is C. Ward (1976) *How to Complain* (London: Pan).

6 Evaluation

Evaluation is the fourth, but not necessarily the final, stage of the problem-solving process. Like assessment, setting objectives, and learning, it is not a finite set of activities sealed off from the others by watertight boundaries of time and place in the programme. It is rather an organic and continuous part of the whole process.

Purposes of evaluation

Evaluation serves two main purposes:

1 it enables individuals to check the progress they are making towards the achievement of their objectives and solutions to some of their personal problems;
2 it provides feedback on the content and effectiveness of programmes so that staff can improve future ones.

At the same time, evaluation procedures should be designed to introduce people to the idea of monitoring their own performance, and should equip them with the skills they require to do it for themselves when tackling subsequent problems.

Chapter aims

The aims of this chapter are:

1 To outline a range of available evaluation methods; and
2 To suggest ways in which they can be used in problem-solving exercises.

The place of evaluation in the programme

Good learning relies heavily on the amount and quality of the information received by the learner about what he is doing. Negative feedback of any kind, from self-dissatisfaction to outright failure in completing a task, can act both as a spur to renewed efforts and as a pointer to what needs to be put right. A recovering alcoholic who gets drunk may feel shame when he admits the fact to other group members. A job applicant who makes a poor showing in an interview can resolve to do better next time by rehearsing the bits he did badly. But a diet of unrelieved criticism will stunt the growth of even the most vigorously motivated person.

Positive feedback or rewards are also needed to reinforce successful learning: a sense of progress in overcoming problems; the pleasure of achievement; the praise of others. It is essential, therefore, that evaluation should not become something tacked

What is to be evaluated?

	Programme	*Members*
Before	Formulation of aims Programme planning Recruitment of members – advertising – selection Staff training	
During	Overall programme *and* individual sessions: – relevance – acceptability – feasibility – effectiveness Staff performance Facilities/resources Staff evaluation of programme and sessions	Enjoyment Individual learning gains – information – attitudes – skills Group cohesion Likes/dislikes Suggested improvements
After		Achievement of short-term goals Progress towards long-term goals Retention of previous learning gains Retrospective judgement of value of course activities

onto the end of the proceedings, but should be seen as a thread running through the whole of the process, activity by activity, session by session, day by day, week by week. This prompts the question: 'What should be evaluated?' The simple answer is 'everything', but a guide to some of the things that should be looked at is set out on page 119.

Each of the items to be evaluated can be expanded into a series of questions to which answers are sought, e.g.

Staff performance: How do staff rate their own performance? How is it rated by group members? Which parts of the programme were they most happy with? Which were the least successful? How could they be improved? Were the sessions properly prepared? Do staff need more practice in some techniques? More information? New material? Better equipment? How did they get on with group members; as a whole/individually? How did they handle conflicts?

Group cohesion: Did the members get on well with each other? If not, what were the sources of conflict? Did members see the group as helpful? Was there a good mixture of problems and personalities? How could selection be improved?

Evaluation methods

Answers to these and other questions can be obtained in a variety of ways. In one sense, evaluation represents the assessment stage turned back on the problem-solving process itself, and any of the methods described in Chapter 3 can be adapted for use in this way. They range fron naive self-report to the re-use, under controlled conditions, of sophisticated psychometric tests; but in most cases evaluation makes use of methods taken from the following list.

1 *Paper-and-pencil methods*
  sentence completion
  written reports
  logs and diaries
  questionnaires
  check lists
  ratings
  rankings
  tests.
2 *Interviews*
  structured
  semi-structured
  unstructured
  peer interviews.

3 *Group discussion*
   combined with other methods, e.g. observation,
   pencil-and-paper.
4 *Observation*
   combined with other methods, e.g. video ratings.

PAPER-AND-PENCIL METHODS

As in assessment, it is the volume and availability of pencil-and-paper methods that threaten to overwhelm this part of the process. They should not, however, be allowed to dominate the actual practice of evaluation, but should take their place alongside interviews, observation, and group discussion, depending on what precisely is being evaluated.

Pencil-and-paper methods can be used effectively to measure gains in information, changes in feelings, and improvements in skill performance; but they should never assume the shape of an impersonal examination. They should have clearly stated aims, be intelligible, acceptable, and useful to users, and they should be applied in moderate doses.

Sentence completion
Sentence completion provides a great deal of information. The sentences may be repetitions of ones used during the assessment stage, or new ones can be devised to check on changes in knowledge, feelings, or abilities.

Knowing

My rights on arrest are . . .
Three places where you can get housing advice are . . .

Feeling

When I go for interviews I will feel . . .
My attitude to gambling is . . .

Doing

I am good at . . .
When I am next stopped by a policeman I will . . .

Written reports, logs, and diaries

A written report can be anything from an answer to the question, 'what are three things you liked/disliked about this course', to personal letters or essays several pages long, and accounts of things like, 'how I found a flat', or 'the steps I took to clear off my biggest debts'. Open-ended responses of this sort are especially good for finding out whether the learning period has helped someone to achieve a long-term objective. And the passage of time also allows individuals to see a course or programme in perspective and to report back a more considered view, weeks or even months after the event.

Even more precise records may be necessary for monitoring specific behaviour changes following the completion of a problem-solving process. For individuals whose personal objectives include things like cutting down on drinking time, or expenditure, or making better use of spare time, diaries or logs can give clear indications of how far they are being achieved.

Questionnaires

A questionnaire format combining different types of item is often the most practical way of gathering information for use in evaluation, and an example of one is given on page 127. It may contain open-ended questions, together with a variety of more structured methods, for example, multiple choice questions, check lists, and rating scales.

Multiple choice questions are most appropriate for testing gains in information. Someone who wants to assess his progress towards understanding consumer rights might wish to answer questions of the following type.

If you sign an HP agreement, how much time do you have to change your mind?

☐ no time
☐ 14 days
☐ 1 month
☐ 3 months

Tick the correct answer.

Check lists are simple to devise, and useful for evaluating a number of things: the achievement of personal objectives, for example, and the success of the programme as a whole. The one below is simply a set of descriptive words.

Ready-made check lists, such as the Mooney, which have been used during the assessment stage, can be completed again during evaluation, and the results compared to see if there has been any progress made during the interval.

How have you found the programme?

☐ useful	☐ interesting	☐ friendly
☐ stressful	☐ uncomfortable	☐ irritating
☐ helpful	☐ supporting	☐ worthwhile
☐ boring	☐ anger-producing	☐ unproductive

Tick the words you agree with.

Rating scales

Rating scales are particularly useful for looking at changes in feelings. Someone trying to improve his ability to initiate conversations with strangers, for instance, can be invited to complete the following rating scale at intervals during the programme.

When I talk to strangers I feel:

tense		————	————	————	————		relaxed
confident		————	————	————	————		not confident
interesting		————	————	————	————		uninteresting
tongue-tied		————	————	————	————		fluent.

This, if the programme is working, will produce a record of growing confidence and capability.

Similar scales can be constructed and applied to almost any personal feeling, attitude, or motive: likes and dislikes, optimism/pessimism, prejudices, anxieties, and self-perceptions. And they can be used as before-and-after measures, and for evaluating responses to programmes and parts of programmes.

How did you find the role-play on family situations?

Useful |————|————|————|————| Not useful

How much have you enjoyed this course?

A lot |————|————|————|————| Not at all

Ranking can also be used to gain some impression of the relative usefulness or acceptability of particular activities, but a straightforward ordering of events does not provide so much detailed information as a rating scale.

Tests

Tests of a more formal nature may be more or less useful depending on what is being evaluated. If areas of knowledge or sets of attitudes have been tested with formal methods during the assessment period then it is quite a good idea to repeat them for evaluation purposes. These can be ready-made, standardized measures such as intelligence tests and personality inventories, or they can be home-made ones.

Whichever they are, they should be treated with the same degree of caution as was advised in the assessment chapter. The results of any single pencil-and-paper measure, no matter how sophisticated or highly regarded it may be, is no basis for drawing sweeping conclusions about what has happened to an individual or how effective a programme is. Such results should always be set alongside others gained in different ways, and tested for consistency. When results do not agree, further methods should be tried until a clearer picture emerges.

INTERVIEWS

Interviews, whether they are unstructured, semi-structured, or structured, are an obvious method for evaluating the success of a problem-solving programme. Just asking direct questions like 'how would you handle that situation now?' or 'how confident are you now about approaching and talking to a woman you do not know?' will provide immediate feedback on individual progress and the overall effectiveness of the programme activities.

At the unstructured end of the range, an evaluation interview might consist of nothing more than a chat over a cup of tea. At the other end it could be a highly organized, market-research type of questionnaire administered verbally. Both sorts can be applied either by staff members or by group members as peer interviews. A check-list interview completed on a peer basis, and handed back to the interviewee, can be a novel alternative to more conventional forms of evaluation. Between these two extremes, an interview plan for a semi-structured interview might look like this:

> *General evaluation interview plan*
>
> Areas to be covered:
> (a) were expectations of the course fulfilled?
> (b) course atmosphere
> (c) relations with staff
> (d) relations with other group members

(e) learning gains
(f) likes/dislikes
(g) outstanding aims
(h) areas not covered
(i) suggestions for improving the course
(j) anything else?

Evaluation interviews should not, however, take place only at the end of a course or programme. They should be written into the timetable as a continuing part of the process. And they should feature in any attempts that are made to find out what long-term effects have been achieved in the period following completion of a course or exercise.

GROUP DISCUSSION

Group discussion tends to generate feedback that is rather too diffuse for proper evaluation purposes, but it is a good starting point. And it is an ideal forum for group members who wish to publicize the degree of progress they have made towards the achievement of some personal objective. In these situations, the immediate feedback given by other group members, based on their knowledge and experience of the individual, can also be invaluable. This is particularly relevant for individuals who are attempting to overcome problems of self-confidence and self-presentation, since other group members will be able to provide informed opinions on their progress based on long periods of contact. But, for other purposes, the views aired during group discussion, unless captured on video- or audio-tape, tend to evaporate fairly quickly, leaving behind only the most general impression of approval or disapproval, or more frequently of indecision. It is nevertheless a good idea to close the proceedings at the end of each session or each day with a brief discussion period in which any member can voice his thoughts and feelings about the doings of the day, about the programme, or about himself or anybody else.

Finally, group discussion by itself is unlikely to yield evaluative data that can be used in isolation, to make decisions either about individuals or about changes in programmes; it should, as far as possible, form part of a process that incorporates many other methods as well.

OBSERVATION

The best way of finding out how well people actually *do* anything is to observe their behaviour. Ideally the behaviour should take place in the real world – at home, at work, in official agencies, during leisure time – and the observer should be some third party such as a relative, friend, or fellow course member who has agreed to help with the evaluation procedure in this way. They can be asked to observe and then record or rate on simple forms and log-sheets any kind of behaviour that an individual is trying to change, from being polite to nosy neighbours to swearing less often, being more assertive with officials, or using the telephone.

The simplest recording of observed behaviour would be a general statement to the effect that: 'John has been trying hard to cut down his drinking and has spent much more time with his pigeons and mending his motorbike than he used to. It seems to have kept him out of the pub more, and he has certainly not asked me for so much money to spend on drink.' More precise records might entail filling in and signing daily or weekly diaries of the relevant behaviour or the completion of 'on-the-spot' rating scales, e.g. for telephone skills.

This may not be possible in some situations, such as claiming benefit at the DHSS, and a friend who accompanies the claimant may need to fill in an evaluation form after the event, or just report his impressions verbally afterwards, either to the individual concerned or to the other members of the group to which they both belong.

Yet other situations cannot be observed by third persons at all, disciplinary interviews, for instance, or encounters likely to lead to fights. In these cases, role-play can serve as a substitute. An individual who wishes to be more polite to traffic wardens, for instance, can role-play what actually transpired the last time he met one and ask other group members to rate and comment on his simulated performance. And the value of video in all of this cannot be over-stressed. It permits the making of permanent records and allows people to gauge progress in any performance area they have chosen to change. Gains in self-confidence and self-presentation skills literally grab the eye on a video screen in a way that is more direct and dramatic than any verbal or written report. Similarly, when groups have grown accustomed to using VTR, the most open-ended method of getting feedback on personal progress and the quality of the programme is to ask individuals to talk directly to the camera, with no-one else present, to say what they think. This will be couched, as often as not, in uncompromising terms – sometimes uncomplimentary, but always useful.

Monitoring the programme

Clearly the most telling evaluation of a programme's effectiveness is provided by concrete achievement in the real world: a job obtained after a long period of unemployment; a period of non-gambling sustained against all the odds; even a date with a desirable girl. Reports like this are good for the individuals concerned and for the groups of which they are members, as well as for the staff who have designed and carried out a programme. Programme staff, both writers and administrators, have a vested interest in the evaluations of their group members, and the methods outlined here provide information on which improvements in content and style of presentation can be based.

The first test of any programme lies in its acceptability to the users. If it falls at that hurdle, the rest of the race is lost almost before it starts. Voluntary attendance provides a brutally direct form of evaluation in this respect; absentees are voting with their feet. With those who remain (and there is no real reason why it should fall much below 100 per cent) the question of acceptability can be raised and answered by most of the evaluation procedures already outlined. Relevance and utility are other qualities that need to be investigated. When working with groups, relevance is a battlefield on which total victory is impossible, since every programme must represent a compromise between the needs of some very different individuals and the construction of a time-table of activities which commands the interest and assent of at least a working majority of the members present.

Another facet of acceptability concerns staff performance, and opportunities should be given for candid comment to be made, either in open session or anonymously, about the way in which sessions have been designed and run. Staff should be warned that wounding criticisms may be made of their personal style, and that groups may occasionally trample on a cherished activity. But, on balance, feedback tends to be good, and the criticisms rational and constructive in character.

An economical way of evaluating personal progress in problem solving, and the effectiveness of the programme, is to combine items dealing with both into a single pencil-and-paper measure, to be used at whatever intervals seem helpful, and which can be supplemented by other methods as necessary.

A basic evaluation form

1. How much have you enjoyed this session/series/programme?

   A lot ⌊___⌊___⌊___⌊___⌊___⌋ Not at all

2. How useful has it been to you?

   Not at all useful ⌊___⌊___⌊___⌊___⌊___⌋ Very useful

3. Rate the following activities for personal usefulness:

   Pencil and paper

   Very useful ⌊___⌊___⌊___⌊___⌊___⌋ Not at all useful

   Role-play

   Very useful ⌊___⌊___⌊___⌊___⌊___⌋ Not at all useful

   Discussion

   Very useful ⌊___⌊___⌊___⌊___⌊___⌋ Not at all useful

   Continued on following page

```
        Interviews
        Very useful      |__|__|__|__|__|__|  Not at all useful
        Lecture
        Very useful      |__|__|__|__|__|__|  Not at all useful
        Films
        Very useful      |__|__|__|__|__|__|  Not at all useful
        Video-tape
        Very useful      |__|__|__|__|__|__|  Not at all useful
4.  How confident are you about solving your problem(s)?
        Very confident   |__|__|__|__|__|__|  Not at all confident
5.  How well do you think the programme has been organized?
6.  How well have the staff done their job?
7.  Write down three things you have liked about the programme.
8.  Write down three things you have disliked about the programme.
9.  What suggestions can you make for improving future programmes?
```

The items in Question 3 have been written in here as 'types' of activity; in an actual evaluation form they would be replaced by specific session titles such as 'job-search simulation', 'role-play of violent incidents', 'speaker on welfare rights', or 'film on jobs in the oil industry'.

With small amendments this sort of form can also be used for follow-up. Sometimes it is only with the passage of time that learning gains make their presence felt in the lives of individuals and it is important, therefore, to keep in touch with them after the completion of a problem-solving exercise. This can be done by sending forms for them to fill in and return, by encouraging them to telephone or write letters, by going to see them and doing an interview, and by organizing follow-up meetings where discussion and pencil-and-paper methods can be deployed.

Completing the cycle

Although evaluation is logically the last of the four problem-solving stages, it is not intended that it should act in any way as a full stop to the process. It should be seen rather as the completion of a cycle of activities in which the results of evaluation have a continuing effect on the assessment, setting objectives, and learning phases that have preceded it.

If an individual has solved his problem to his own satisfaction then the process has

A problem-solving cycle

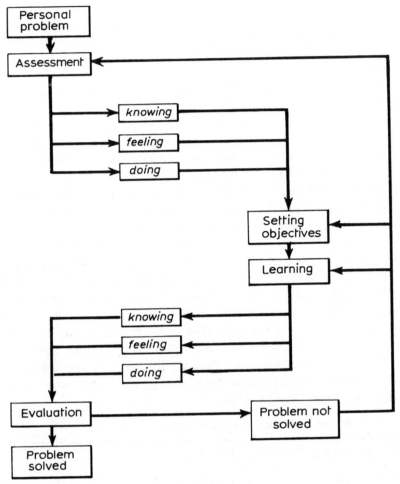

done its job, and evaluation is needed only to provide positive feedback to all concerned, and to pinpoint places where the programme could still be improved. But if the
problem is not solved (and staff members need not fear imminent unemployment
when they use this approach) then the cycle can be used to indicate where things went
wrong. It may be that assessment should be gone over again, reviewing material
already assembled, exploring new areas using different methods, or approaching the
problem from a different perspective altogether. Possibly, the assessment has not been
at fault, but the wrong objectives have been set, and new ones may need to be
formulated and pursued. Alternatively, defective learning may be to blame, and may
need to be repeated or added to in some way. In any of these cases, the cycle can be

re-entered at the appropriate point and the process reworked until a better solution is achieved.

One last point needs to be made about this part of the process. The adoption of an explicit problem-solving approach and the use of terms like 'evaluation' invites comparison with the accuracy and strict criteria of success demanded by the scientific method proper. Do the results that emerge from the application of the methods described in this book measure up to these sternly objective standards? Strictly speaking the answer must be 'no'. During their translation from 'pure science' the commonsense stages of the problem-solving cycle have become personalized. At every stage – defining the problem, setting objectives, learning, and evaluation – the significance and the meaning of all the activities have been subjected to the personal judgement of the participants rather than that of the 'experts'.

This is not meant to imply that most people have a totally idiosyncratic view of themselves and their place in the world; on the contrary, even when pressured by the most awful personal problems, most people seem to retain a healthy objectivity which should be encouraged and strengthened. It should never be set aside in favour of some supposedly scientific notion of validity. The variety of methods employed at every stage permit the participant to view himself and his problems from a multitude of angles and in a number of overlapping dimensions. Somewhere in the middle of all this is something that approximates to the reality being experienced by the person with the problem. Similarly, with any solutions that might be arrived at, it is, in the final analysis, the user of the methods who must pronounce on their effectiveness. His evidence about his own problem is, after all, the most powerful justification for undertaking problem-solving programmes in the first place, and he must have the last word on how successful they have been.

Evaluation methods: section of the curriculum matrix

	Knowing	*Feeling*	*Doing*
Evaluation	Post-tests on similar scales or other measures Interviews	Rating scales Final or follow-up interviews Self-report Group discussion	Goal achievement Diaries Self-presentation Observation of behaviour

Note: see page 139 for the completed curriculum matrix

Notes and references

Social work has no real tradition of evaluating its own efforts, and there are no readily available references to be recommended. There are, however, general texts in the field, e.g. E. J. Mullen and J. R. Dumpson (1972) *Evaluation of Social Intervention* (San

Francisco: Jossey-Bass), and R. Lees (1975) *Research Strategies for Social Welfare* (London: Routledge and Kegan Paul). And for a pessimistic account of evaluation studies in criminology, see S. R. Brody (1976) *The Effectiveness of Sentencing*, Home Office Research Study No. 35 (London: HMSO).

But for practical purposes we suggest that workers adopt a do-it-yourself attitude to the construction of workable evaluation measures. The aim, after all, is not to produce statistically impregnable research findings, but to help people with problems check on the progress they are making and to give staff members feedback on their own performance so that they can improve it. Anything at all that serves these two purposes should be used. The assessment section of this book may be ransacked for ideas, as well as the whole literature on the subject that lies behind it. But, as with the rest of the approach, the techniques should be retained for future use only if they survive the trial of common sense and the ordeal of customer approval.

3 Programmes and applications

7 Programme construction

By five past midnight, Cinderella had precious little left to remind her of the glories of the ball. Helping other people is often like that, too; apart from a possible epitaph in the case notes, the shape and content of the helping encounter pass quickly beyond all possible hope of reconstruction. This is partly due to the elusive nature of much human interaction. But it is also a product of styles of working in which the ends of the endeavour are less than clear to both participants, and the means of achieving them sometimes obscured by jargon and bureaucratic procedure.

The approach proposed in this book points in the opposite direction: to the creation of written programmes of activities dealing explicitly with specific problems, such as money, work, or accommodation. These programmes have unambiguous aims and clear methods, and they summarize activities from each of the four stages of the problem-solving process. They represent a kind of badge or symbol of the whole approach in action and they encapsulate the idea of a curriculum for the practice of helping people directly with their problems. But their relative novelty should not deter anyone from attempting to work in this way. Almost anyone who wishes to can construct workable programmes for use with both individuals and groups. This 'do-it-yourself' dimension has been stressed throughout the book and is one of several that characterize the business of programme construction. Another is flexibility, since the programme is not intended to become just another strait-jacket on practice. Its purpose is to provide an infinitely adaptable framework within which almost any method, piece of material, or personal resource can be pressed into service to help someone solve a problem. And since the sources of such methods and materials are almost limitless it follows that the programme is not a static entity but a growing and changing repertory of practical things to do. Programmes ought also to have the virtue of 'transferability', drawing as they do on the work of many minds and the collective experience of many workers, and taking the form of simple session plans within the stages of the problem-solving process. Ideally, every written programme should be constructed in such a way that other workers can take it 'off the shelf' and use it with a minimum of time and preparation.

One way of conceptualizing programmes is to see them, together with the four stages of the process and the division of problems into *knowing*, *feeling*, and *doing* elements, as a kind of grammar which can be acquired by anybody and used to create and re-create utterly distinctive patterns of activity in whatever situation they seek to work. They constitute, in other words, a set of generative rules with practically unbounded possibilities for expression.

Chapter aims

The aims of this chapter are to:

1 outline the process of building programmes,
2 provide examples of programme summaries, and
3 suggest some sources of materials.

The elements of a programme

Written programmes contain seven kinds of ingredient, namely:

1 programme aims
2 stimulus materials
3 assessment methods
4 objective setting
5 learning procedures
6 evaluation methods and
7 resources.

PROGRAMME AIMS

Most programmes are designed to deal with one particular problem area, such as 'rights' or 'leisure', so for each one it is vital to state what the programme seeks to achieve and for whom. The programme aims will be more general or specific depending on the scope of the proposed programme. The aim of a Telephone Use Programme may be 'to enable individuals to use the telephone more effectively', whereas that of a

Work Programme may be 'to look at some problems to do with finding and keeping jobs'. The general programme aims will be narrowed down to individual goals in the course of setting objectives as part of the problem-solving process. In some cases, where a group of individuals with the same specific problem are gathered together, the programme aims can be quite clear and succinct: for example, for a group of problem drinkers, the overall aim of an Alcohol Programme could be 'to enable group members to stop or reduce their drinking'. In this case individual objectives will relate to possible ways of attaining the overall aim of the programme.

Programme aims are not difficult to formulate for any kind of problem area, but their importance for all concerned would be difficult to over-estimate; they represent the terms of reference for staff and participants alike, and the simpler and more forceful they can be made the less likely it is that confusion will arise at any point about what is being attempted. They should also feature prominently in any advertising that is undertaken to attract group members.

STIMULUS MATERIAL

Even when people have been recruited and assembled on the basis of a self-perceived problem, it may still be necessary to stimulate some initial interest in the topic that is to be tackled by the programme. Stimulus materials comprise anything at all that can serve this purpose. It might be a film, e.g. *Gale is Dead* for a drug abuse programme, *Edna the Inebriate Woman* for alcohol, or *Cathy Come Home* for accommodation. Less dramatic but equally stimulating might be the presentation of a case history illustrating a personal problem, with money or embarrassment or anything else, delivered either by a staff member or, better still, by the person with the problem. Speakers, video-tapes, cartoons, simulations, role-plays, personal statements – the range of possible stimulus materials is vast. The only tests for inclusion are relevance and effectiveness, which will become evident in the course of repeated use. It is useful to have two or three possible stimulus items available for any one programme.

ASSESSMENT METHODS

Every programme should contain a variety of assessment methods relevant to its aims. Every individual who uses it will be different and should be given an opportunity to choose from a variety of paths through the problem-solving process. The methods themselves will be of two sorts. One group will consist of what might be called 'standard methods' drawn from some of those described in the assessment chapter, and including things like sentence completion, pattern notes, check lists, rating scales, interviews, group discussion, and observation, any of which can be applied in any context with very little preparation. The remainder will be specially devised or highly specific assessment tools: a copyrighted intelligence test or personality inventory or attitude scale, for example, dealing with the subject in hand, be it aggression, sex, or assertiveness. Or they could be specially designed role-plays or observation exercises. Some examples will be given in the outline programmes later in this chapter.

SETTING OBJECTIVES

Most of the methods presented in the chapter on setting personal objectives are 'standard methods' which require little adaptation for use in any programme, the exception being check lists of specimen objectives, which have to be constructed afresh for use with particular problems.

LEARNING PROCEDURES

Even more than assessment, learning is a growth area for programme writers and developers. Potential material of all kinds is available in profusion almost everywhere you care to look, in the form of information, personal expertise, and techniques and ideas in education, training, and social work. Some of it can be used with little or no modification; some of it has to be worked on. Some suggestions about where to look for new material are made in the section on *Resources* which follows.

EVALUATION

In many cases the criterion for the achievement of an objective will be quite obvious, e.g. finding out certain facts. In other cases, objectives may be set which require more sophisticated measures of confidence or performance. Whichever is the case, the programme should contain evaluation procedures relevant to the sorts of objectives likely to be set during its course. Once again, the more a programme is used the more useful will be the evaluation procedures that emerge.

In each of the four 'process' chapters, a mixture of standard methods and specific activities have been described and then summarized in terms of the *knowing*, *feeling*, and *doing* classification which runs through the book. These are brought together below in a completed form of the curriculum matrix which was drawn empty in the first chapter. The entries represent cryptic titles for resources beyond the scope of a single book.

Resources

One last item completes the list of programme ingredients: that of resources. In the concrete sense this entails making a list of those people, facilities, materials, and pieces

A curriculum matrix for social work: some standard methods

	Knowing	*Feeling*	*Doing*
Assessment	Tests, essays, exams, check lists, information-gathering interviews, situation tests	Questionnaires, rating scales, sentence completion, projective techniques, pattern notes, group discussion, counselling, self-report, introspection	Task performance and observation, skill analysis, life histories, role-play, fishbowl groups, 'objective' measures
Setting objectives	Check lists of specimen objectives, profiles of problem areas, sentence completion, wall charts, individual learning contracts, cards, counselling and co-counselling, group discussion		
Learning procedures	Direct teaching, hand-outs, lectures, visits, libraries, resource centres, programmed learning, individual learning packages, vocational guidance, projects	Confrontation, group-work of many kinds, role-play, counselling, 'positive strokes', trust exercises, encouragement	Modelling, rehearsal, practice, simulation, critical incidents analysis, successive approximation, problem-solving procedures, information search
Evaluation	Post-tests on similar scales or other measures, interviews	Rating scales, final or follow-up interviews, self-report, group discussion	Goal achievement, diaries, self-presentation, observation of behaviour

of equipment that are needed to run a programme. But resources also make their presence felt throughout the four stages of the problem-solving process, as a repository of possible things to do and of places to look for more. The following examples may be useful in providing ideas and possible content areas for the construction of programmes.

(a) *Resources for assessment/self-assessment*: tests, questionnaires, inventories, scales, check lists, forms, or just blank sheets of paper for people to write on. Apart from the 'pencil-and-paper' kinds of assessment there are also interviews, peer interviews, group discussions, brainstorming sessions, critical incidents analysis, reactions to case histories and video.

(b) *Resources for teaching/learning*: refer to any method that helps to induce or support change at any level: direct teaching, projects, counselling, goal analysis, setting behavioural objectives, successive approximation, practice, experiential learning, discovery learning, programmed learning texts, self-organized learning modules, client-centred therapy, and, of course, personal contact itself.

(c) *Games*: using this word in a broad sense, it can cover anything from the mildly engaging to the totally involved. Thus we can include co-operation games, competitions, simulations, imitation, modelling, role-plays, or psychodrama.

(d) *Educational and informational resources*: this is probably the most obvious (even taken-for-granted) category, including books and papers from colleges and libraries; information leaflets from all central and local government departments; pamphlets from charities, pressure groups, and voluntary organizations; regular publications of these and many other bodies (journals, bulletins, newsletters, catalogues); and book lists and periodicals of the Schools Council, Open University, ILEA Media Resources Centre, and many more.

(e) *Visual and audiovisual aids*: these may include anything from blackboards and flipcharts to posters, tapes, overhead projectors, video, or radio and TV broadcasts. Sources for these or for the hire of films, displays, and so on might include the BBC, National Audio-Visual Aids Centre, Educational Foundation for Visual Aids, or the Training Boards of many industries. Arts and crafts materials of many kinds can also be useful in this respect.

(f) *Groupwork*: apart from the group discussion which takes place both formally and informally, the use of groupwork in different ways can also be a resource in itself. Variations might include large 'parent' groups; smaller groups for 'syndicate' work; dyads, triads, or the 'group-on-group'; and changes in the type of leadership, and in communication patterns in groups.

(g) *The local area*: places and events in the immediate neighbourhood will obviously be more interesting to people than those which are out of reach. A focus on local history, government, newspapers, entertainments, special events, social services, employment, community, and so on, provides abundant resources virtually on the doorstep. Visits are especially valuable in this respect.

(h) *People* – the key resource: apart from staff and course members themselves, and the personal resources they can bring to the group, there are many links with outside people which can be useful: for example, with local representatives of any government department, Jobcentre, Skillcentre, DHSS, Police, Alcoholics Anonymous, Small Firms Information Centre, voluntary bodies, trade unions, Workers' Educational Association, or Citizens Advice Bureau; and links and/or exchanges with people in other places pursuing goals similar to, or related to, those of your group. All of these and others may be willing to give talks or demonstrations, or provide information.

(i) *Organization*: besides all of the above, and a lot more not mentioned, another major resource is the manner in which you organize the resources you already have. This might be in the construction of a 'curriculum' in the broad sense, in the preparation of simple programmes, in helping individuals with projects of their own, and in the allocation of staff roles.

Some uses of video

A resource that is worthy of special note here is that of video. Video has two principal assets for social skills and personal problem solving: first, its impact on individuals in allowing them to see themselves 'as others see them'; and, second, its flexibility, which makes it invaluable as a tool at every stage of problem solving and programme construction. The effects of video must by now be legendary – like the shock of hearing one's own recorded voice for the first time, but with a greatly magnified effect. Initial reactions to video are extremely variable, and can range from fits of nervous laughter to instant recoil and fright. It is perhaps because many users never go beyond this stage that video has acquired a reputation in some places as being little more than a 'toy'. In fact, as a means of making learning more enjoyable, absorbing, and likely to last, it is difficult to surpass.

It is from the ability to provide *feedback* that video derives some of its key uses, particularly in social skills training. Normal feedback on social behaviour is indirect, long-winded, and often distorted by convention and politeness. Video feedback on the other hand can be immediate and brutally true to real life; it is therefore able to furnish individuals with a window on themselves, a position from which they can assess, improve, and evaluate their own social performance in the most direct manner possible. And this is true for a whole range of skills, from saying 'hello' to negotiating difficult conflicts and emerging unscathed.

Another prime use to which video can be put is as an *information-giving* medium. Lectures by experts who cannot afford the time to repeat their performances *in vivo* (or whose fees are too high), can be recorded and used again. Similarly, the presentation of almost any item of information can be enhanced and made more interesting if recorded on video.

Coupled with this are the possibilities that video presents for the mounting of *projects*. The filming of role-plays, the making of a film about some topic of interest, the recording of street interviews on a controversial subject, or any other learning project can have great benefits for users of video in terms of increased confidence, skills, and social awareness.

Finally, video has a host of applications for all the elements of a programme described earlier in this chapter. A talk, role-play, or opening group discussion recorded on tape provides a striking stimulus and seems capable of holding the attention longer, oddly enough, than most people 'in the flesh'. During assessment, video can be put to many uses: for recording peer interviews or personal introductions;

The uses of video: some possibilities

Some of the suggestions included below require prior preparation of a tape for a specific purpose; others are examples of 'on-the-spot' use to provide immediate feedback of some kind, for assessment, learning, or evaluation.

Relaying or recording information

1 Presenting the aims of an agency to the public, or to other agencies.
2 Making a directory of staff members and their interests.
3 Recruitment tapes for staff or course members.
4 Descriptions of agency resources.
5 Sources of help in the local community.
6 Specially prepared tapes, e.g. on the DHSS, accommodation, work, health problems, parenting, or appearing in court.
7 Reports on staff projects, conferences, etc.

Working with individuals and groups

1 Case recording.
2 Self-assessment – of appearance, interacting with others, etc.
3 Giving and receiving feedback on interview performance, telephone skills, group behaviour.
4 Social skills training exercises, including role-plays, self-presentations, and critical incidents analysis.
5 Modelling tapes of particular skills: the building up of a library of such tapes.
6 Simulations.
7 Group or individual projects: to make a 'profile' of a group; to compile an information tape on some topic; to carry out street interviews; to send video letters to other groups; to record predictions about the future; to do a 'whispers' exercise.
8 Evaluation interviews or self-reports.

Staff training

1 Taped lectures by outside speakers.
2 Feedback on interview technique.
3 Case illustrations.
4 Tapes about agency procedures.
5 Training projects and reports on them.

for observational purposes in assessments of social skill or other pieces of behaviour; or for recording the verdict of groups on the value of a particular assessment method. Similarly, in setting objectives, the commitment of a statement about personal goals onto tape adds a strong element of encouragement to the pursuit of such goals. For learning, video can add an additional dimension to any exercise, as well as being an essential element of many social skills training methods, problem-solving exercises, and simulations. Finally, some methods of evaluation make direct use of video – for recording and obtaining feedback on performance, for example; but it can also be used here to make a record of individual or group views on the whole of a programme or course, or to store predictions for the future. The accompanying box points the way towards some other potential applications.

This list of possible resources is incomplete in many ways, but it should be treated as a collection of signposts to other unexplored areas. And whatever is discovered in any environment whatsoever should be plagiarized, adapted, and exploited for use with the people you are helping to solve their personal problems. If they are arranged roughly in the way that has just been suggested, tried in practice, and then polished a little, they will soon come to resemble the kinds of well-constructed, practicable, and effective programme that achieve real results. It is not necessary to be a literary giant in order to do this; and even people without formal qualifications have been known to produce quite excellent examples. Programme writing introduces, in fact, dimensions of creativity and of co-operation with colleagues that are not normally present in much of the work that goes on in helping agencies.

Some examples of programme outlines are given below, and similar ones can be put together in a very short time, an hour or two at the most; the fine detail can be added later. Try it for yourself and see how easy, interesting, and satisfying it can be.

---

1 Job Search Programme Outline

OVERALL PROGRAMME AIMS

To look at group members' work problems, with particular reference to finding and holding jobs.

STIMULUS

1 A film about jobs or about unemployment
2 A role-play on 'why I got the sack'
3 A speaker from the Jobcentre or a particular area of work.

Continued overleaf

ASSESSMENT

This is designed to enable individuals to look at their experience, interests, and aptitudes, and their strengths and weaknesses, and to define more clearly their plans or problems in relation to work. Such problems might include being jobless, having difficulty holding on to jobs, needing to know more about training, wanting to find out about redundancy, having poor or non-existent interview skills, and so on. Assessment tries to find out as much about these and related problems as possible.

Materials to be used might therefore include:

- differential aptitude tests
- work problem check list
- vocational preference forms
- saleable skills form
- knowledge tests
- cartoons depicting problems at work and group discussions
- structured role-plays on 'conflict at work'
- sentence completion, brainstorming, pattern notes
- individual job histories
- observation of interview performance and rating exercises
- peer interview sessions
- occupational guidance interviews.

SETTING OBJECTIVES

Here individuals are helped to identify changes they could make in relation to at least one problem with work. Methods that could be used include:

- a check list of specimen objectives
- wall charts
- counselling sessions.

Examples of possible objectives might be:

- to get a job in a specific area
- to earn more money
- to find out about machine tool jobs in a local area
- to explore the setting up of a small business
- to control one's temper with foremen
- to get a place on a training course.

Continued on following page

LEARNING

Learning procedures to help group members achieve their objectives could include:

- vocational guidance materials such as *Signposts*, *CODOT*, and *Speedcop*
- how to locate job vacancies
- use of telephone
- letter-writing practice
- job interview role-play
- simulation of the process of job search
- speakers, films, or leaflets on jobs or aspects of work (e.g. rights at work, safety, and redundancy)
- programmed learning on some basic job information
- group discussions or personal counselling
- projects for individuals on given work areas
- visits to factories, Jobcentres, or Skillcentres.

EVALUATION

While in many cases the criterion for the achievement of an objective may be obvious (e.g. whether or not someone gets a job or a training place) in other cases it may be less so and may need to be determined from, for example, confidence ratings, observed interview performance, or changes in attitudes to others at work. Interview and group discussion will also be important.

2 Alcohol Programme Outline

OVERALL PROGRAMME AIMS

To explore the problem of alcohol and to provide opportunities for learning ways of changing or coping better with drinking behaviour, either one's own or that of others.

STIMULUS

- a film on the effects of alcoholism
- a recovering alcoholic giving his life story
- a group discussion on 'what drink does to me'.

ASSESSMENT

- Alcoholics Anonymous drinking scale   *Continued overleaf*

- 'what it costs' – drinking bills for a day/week/month/year/lifetime
- the hidden costs of drink
- a drinking history form
- a weekly drinking diary
- drink problems check list
- knowledge quiz on effects of alcohol
- calculating personal blood alcohol levels
- 'my drinking and my family': video self-presentation
- pattern notes on 'drink in my life'.

SETTING OBJECTIVES

Methods:

- counselling
- wall charts
- check lists of specimen objectives
- group discussion.

Possible objectives:

- to stop drinking altogether
- to reduce drinking
- to change drinking habits, times, venues, companions
- to spend less money on drink
- to stop drinking and driving
- to find out about treatment facilities
- to go out later each evening
- to find out what drink does to the body.

LEARNING

- information: legal, medical, social
- relaxation techniques
- self-control methods
- role-plays: refusing a drink/coping with a drunk
- successive approximation to new habits
- alternatives to drink, e.g. leisure pursuits/evening classes
- modelling good behaviour
- demonstration of home-brewing methods
- films and speakers

Continued on following page

- visits to treatment facilities
- projects on the prevalence of alcohol abuse, the economics of drink, licensing laws, etc.

EVALUATION

- self-perception scales
- self-report methods/logs/diaries, etc.
- third-person reports
- changes in habits and related areas, e.g. social life, spending, leisure pursuits
- interviews
- group discussion
- follow-up meetings.

3 Rights Programme Outline

OVERALL PROGRAMME AIMS

To look at group members' problems with welfare, legal, and consumer rights and enable them to acquire knowledge, attitude, and behaviour changes that would help them meet their needs.

STIMULUS

- a speaker from the Citizens Advice Bureau or Child Poverty Action Group
- a film on citizens' rights
- posters and wall charts
- a case history.

ASSESSMENT

- knowledge of the law test
- 'would you know what to do' check list
- self-presentation in crucial areas, e.g. with the DHSS, making consumer complaints
- role-play of behaviour, e.g. on arrest, in court
- brainstorming rights problems.

Continued overleaf

SETTING OBJECTIVES

Examples:

- to be more assertive
- to learn how to fill in forms
- to join a trade union
- to find out about a point of law.

LEARNING

- critical incidents analysis
- role-plays/modelling assertive behaviour at the DHSS/in court
- rehearsing complaining methods
- speakers from helping agencies
- rights booklets and guides
- information search procedures
- making sample 'small claims'
- compiling a 'consumer rights' library.

EVALUATION

- ability to explain points to someone else
- self-report/video performance
- confidence scales
- awarded damages
- obtaining legal aid, money back, etc.

Session plans

These three illustrations give a reasonable idea of what programme outlines look like. But they are not precise recipes to be followed to the letter, either on the topics they deal with, or on any others. Quite different but equally viable and attractive programmes could be constructed for all three titles. And, however they started off, they would in any case grow and change with use.

Nor are they fully written in this form. Many of the items in the outline need to be expanded into session plans describing activities in detail. Sessions can be divided broadly into three types. The 'free-form' session occurs when a group member or the group as a whole has something which must be dealt with without delay, or when a staff member opens the proceedings with the question, 'what is the problem?', and works his way informally into the more structured parts of the programme. For those who feel comfortable and confident in these circumstances, this can be a particularly rewarding way of working. Others will prefer to start in a more organized way, permitting the structure to fade into the background as the group members get hold of the topic and make it their own. A 'semi-structured' session of this sort could begin with a stimulus, such as a film or role-play, followed by discussion. Other activities can then be introduced at appropriate points, and the staff member may have in mind an exercise with which to round off the session.

Yet other sessions will be of necessity highly 'structured' ones. Pencil-and-paper tests fall most easily into this category, but some role-plays and simulations are also by their very nature organized activities. The degree of structure in sessions should not be thought of as constituting a hierarchy of desirability or skill; most programmes will need to make use of all three types. It is up to staff and members to decide what works best for them.

For the most structured activities it is helpful to draw up a simple session plan:

Session plan

1 Aims
2 Materials needed
3 Organization of session
4 Discussion points
5 Conclusion/summary

USING THE TELEPHONE

This is an example of a completed session plan.

Session title	Answering the telephone.
Aims	To illustrate that certain skills are required in answering the telephone in differing situations.
Materials needed	Two linked telephone extensions. Video- or tape-recorders.
Organization of session	This exercise can be carried out with the whole group or individually. Each group member is to imagine himself in the situations listed below. His words and manner in answering the telephone can be recorded on video-tape or audio-tape.

(a) You are answering your personal phone at home.
(b) You work for Rank Services and you are working the switchboard.
(c) You are alone in the Works Manager's office when the phone rings.   *Continued overleaf*

> (d) You are in a friend's house when the phone rings.
>
> (e) You have just entered a call box when the phone inside rings.
>
> When each person has completed the exercise, the group can reconvene and discuss individual styles of answering and their effectiveness.
>
> *Discussion points*   Points to emphasize:
>
> (a) Different words and manner are required in each situation. The amount of information that has to be given varies.
>
> (b) There are no set words to use when answering the telephone, but some phrases are better than others.
>
> (c) Never say 'hello' unless there is some doubt as to whether you are connected.
>
> *Conclusion/summary*   Attempt to obtain a group consensus of opinion on the best way of answering in each situation. Summarize the session and conclude by emphasizing that there is an art to answering the telephone which can be learnt. Were the objectives of the session met?

No matter what the nature of the session, it is a good idea to write up its aims and display them where everyone can see them, preferably alongside the aims of the whole programme to which the session belongs. This not only meets the criterion of explicitness, it also establishes a clear learning destination against which the value of the session can be assessed when it has been completed.

With transient or uniquely assembled groups it is possible to treat a single session in isolation as 'the programme'. One session on job search or accommodation is better than nothing at all. Similarly, there are groups whose members will be interested in completing only a single programme, such as 'Meeting People' or 'Dealing with Debt'. But a more typical problem-solving exercise would involve the use of materials from several programmes, interlinked to cover a number of problem areas. This might best begin with a series of open-ended assessment sessions during which a broad outline of the group's problems can be drawn. Activities of an appropriate kind can then be formulated around this agenda, mixing sessions on different topics to compose an interesting and varied programme. Some outlines of courses organized in this way will be presented in Chapter 8.

Within this kind of mixed curriculum, care should be taken to keep the progression from assessment to evaluation, via objectives and learning procedures, firmly in the minds of group members. And the experience of each participant should be recorded as fully as possible in his personal file. At the end of the proceedings he should be able to retain the file and its contents as a record of what he has learnt and as something to which reference can be made at any subsequent time of difficulty.

Beyond the programme

Programmes are both a storehouse of past learning experiences and a seed-bed for future ones: a bridge between proven utility and continuing innovation. No programme can ever be regarded as a finished article; as in assessment, it is always something that is 'in progress'. In this context, evaluation is a lever with which the consumer makes changes in the problem-solving curriculum.

But even more direct contributions to programmes can be made by their users. In some problem areas the learning part of the process is extended into project work, resulting in the production of immediately usable materials, such as surveys of job opportunities, attitudes, or the prevalence of personal problems in given populations. Or groups of participants may collaborate in making a film which can be used to illustrate a problem and some solutions to it, or in inventing an assessment or learning exercise. Nor is there any reason why some individuals should not undertake substantial responsibility for writing their own programmes, and then working their way through them when, where, and how they please.

As experience is gained in applying this approach to helping people solve their problems, agencies and workers will find that they develop comprehensive libraries of programmes ready for use at a moment's notice, if necessary. They will also find that they can swap programmes and parts of programmes with others who are working in the same way.

Notes and references

The source material for this chapter is organized into several batches, which correspond to some of the most commonly encountered areas of personal problems. Within each area there is a separate listing of books and other usable materials, and of addresses where more of these, and many other kinds of help, may be obtained. Obviously the areas chosen are by no means exhaustive; neither are the suggestions given under each.

GENERAL

Some useful general points about learning, and about the construction of 'packages' into some kind of (problem-solving) curriculum, are made in the following: J. Bruner (1966) *Towards a Theory of Instruction* (Cambridge, Massachusetts: Harvard University

152   Social skills and personal problem solving

Press); and G. A. Beauchamp (1975) *Curriculum Theory* (Wilmette, Illinois: The Kagg Press).

A source of curriculum materials is the Schools Council for Curriculum and Examinations, 160 Great Portland St., London W1.

A good introduction to the many uses of video is M. Murray (1975) *The Videotape Book* (New York: Bantam Books).

Invaluable as general guides to sources of help, and other addresses, are: *Directory of Projects* (annual; Chichester, Sussex: Barry Rose) for adult offenders, alcoholics, drugtakers, homeless single people, and people with histories of mental illness; and C. Moorhead (1975) *Helping – A Guide to Voluntary Work* (London: Macdonald and Jane's).

EMPLOYMENT AND UNEMPLOYMENT

Books and materials
G. Golzen and P. Plumbley (1971) *Changing Your Job* (London: Kogan Page).
B. Hopson and P. Hough (1973) *Exercises in Personal and Career Development* (Cambridge: CRAC).
P. Kinnersley (1973) *The Hazards of Work: How to Fight Them*, Worker's Handbook No. 1 (London: Pluto Press).
P. Laurie (1976) *On the Dole: Your Guide to Unemployment Benefit and Other Things You Need To Know* (London: Kogan Page).
R. Miller (1978) *Equal Opportunities – A Careers Guide for Women and Men* (5th edition; Harmondsworth: Penguin).
P. O'Higgins (1975) *Workers' Rights* (London: Arrow Books/Society of Industrial Tutors).
Opportunities for School Leavers (annual; London: New Opportunities Press): this is a directory of jobs for young people, in four volumes: South, Midlands, North, and Scotland; it may be found in the local careers library.
E. Rudinger (ed.) (1976) *Dismissal, Redundancy and Job Hunting* (London: Consumers' Association).
T. Topham (1975) *The Organized Worker* (London: Arrow Books/Society of Industrial Tutors).
C. Ward (1972) *Work* ('Connexions' series; Harmondsworth: Penguin).

Also useful are the vocational guidance materials – *Signposts, Speedcop, CODOT* – mentioned under that section of the sources for Chapter 5.

The setting up of a job-search simulation, a valuable component of a programme on work problems, requires only minimal resources: pencils and paper with which to write 'job ads' and letters of application; possibly a 'telephone skills' exercise; and a small group to simulate job interviews, with perhaps other individuals as observers or (if possible) video cameramen. An 'Appointments Board' simulation is available as No.

5 in the series of nine provided by the ILEA Learning Materials Service, Highbury Station Road, London N1 1SB.

Addresses
A great deal of information on jobs is obviously available in the local newspapers, Jobcentres, and Offices of the Department of Employment and the Training Services Agency. The last of these will also be able to supply information about vocational training courses available in government Skillcentres, and addresses of the training boards that exist for numerous industries.

The Careers and Occupational Information Centre, 3 St. Andrews Place, London NW1, publishes an *Annual Careers Guide* which you can obtain directly from them. It also produces the Connolly Occupational Interests Questionnaire.

Central Office of the Industrial Tribunals, 93 Ebury Bridge Road, London SW1S 8RE, and St. Andrews House, 141 West Nile Street, Glasgow G1 2RU.

National Institute of Careers Education and Counselling, Bateman Street, Cambridge CB2 1LZ.

Small Firms Information Centres are situated in each region of the country (in London, Luton, Bristol, Cardiff, Birmingham, Nottingham, Manchester, Leeds, Newcastle, and Glasgow); information can also be obtained from Small Firms Division, Department of Industry, Abell House, John Islip Street, London SW1P 4LN.

Trades Union Congress (TUC), Congress House, 23–8 Great Russell Street, London WC1.

ACCOMMODATION

Books and materials
Ron Bailey (1973) *The Squatters* (Harmondsworth: Penguin) and (1977) *The Homeless and the Empty Houses* (Harmondsworth: Penguin).

D. Watkinson and M. Reed (1976) *Squatting, Trespass, and Civil Liberties* (London: National Council for Civil Liberties).

A simulated 'accommodation search' can also be mounted with very limited resources, involving advertisements for accommodation (obtained from newspapers or simply made up), forms to fill in (from the Local Authority Housing Department or Town Hall), and role-played interviews between landlord and tenant, etc. Note also that simulations are available from the Shelter Community Education Programme (see references to Chapter 5).

Addresses
Advisory Service for Squatters, 2 St. Paul's Road, London N1.

Campaign for the Homeless and Rootless (CHAR), 27 Endell Street, London WC2.

Shelter Housing Aid Centre, 189a Old Brompton Road, London SW10.

Shelter, National Campaign for the Homeless, 157 Waterloo Road, London SE1 8UU.

A great deal of other information, e.g. on rights to home repairs, rent rebates, transfers of accommodation, is available in leaflet form from the Local Authority, or local Housing Aid or Housing Advice Centre.

MONEY

Books and materials

C. Adams, S. Gagg, and G. Tayar (1973, 1974) *Living Decisions in Family and Community* (Vols. 1 and 2; London: BBC Publications).

M. Allen (1971) *The Save and Prosper Book of Money* (London: Dale/Collins).

J. Blamire and A. Izzard (1975) *Debt Counselling* (Birmingham: Birmingham Settlement Money Advice Centre).

Fair Deal – A Shopper's Guide (1978) (revised edition; London: Office of Fair Trading).

E. A. Gundray (1975) *Making Ends Meet: A Practical Guide to Family Finance* (London: Arrow Books).

T. Lynes (1975) *Penguin Guide to Supplementary Benefits* (3rd edition; Harmondsworth: Penguin).

E. Rudinger (ed.) (1975) *How to Sue in the County Court* (London: Consumers' Association).

Supplementary Benefits Handbook (periodically revised; London: HMSO).

H. Toch (1977) *How to Survive Inflation* (London: Pitman Publishing).

A. Williams (1975) *Educating the Consumer – A Practical Guide* (Harlow: Longman).

Addresses

Birmingham Settlement Money Advice Centre, 318 Summer Lane, Birmingham B19 3RL.

Charity Commission, 14 Ryder Street, London SW1.

Child Poverty Action Group, 1 Macklin Street, London WC2 – also has local branches in many parts of the country, producing amongst other things booklets describing the main financial provisions available to those in need in the particular area.

Consumers' Association, 14 Buckingham Street, London WC2 – publishers of *Which?*, a monthly guide to more effective buying.

Gamblers Anonymous, 17–23 Blantyre Street, London SW10.

Good Housekeeping Institute, Chestergate House, Vauxhall Gate Road, London SW1V 1HF.

National Federation of Consumer Groups, 61 Valentine Road, Birmingham B14
     7AJ.
Office of Fair Trading, Field House, Breams Buildings, London EC4.

FAMILY AND RELATED PROBLEMS

Books and materials
C. Adams, S. Gagg, and G. Tayar (1973, 1974) *Living Decisions in Family and Community*
     (Vols. 1 and 2; London: BBC Publications).
A. Coote and T. Gill (1977) *Women's Rights, A Practical Guide* (Harmondsworth: Pen-
     guin).
J. Dominian (1968) *Marital Breakdown* (Harmondsworth: Penguin).
C. Hannam (1976) *Parents and Mentally Handicapped Children* (Harmondsworth: Pen-
     guin/MIND).
M. Herbert (1976) *Problems of Childhood* (London: Corgi Books).
B. and C. Hopson (1973) *Twosome Plus: A Guide to Cohabitation with Exercises* (London:
     Blond and Briggs).
M. Laufer (1976) *Adolescent Disturbance and Breakdown* (Harmondsworth: Pen-
     guin/MIND).
E. Rudinger (ed.) (1976) *Getting a Divorce* (London: Consumers' Association).
M. L. Rutter (1975) *Helping Troubled Children* (Harmondsworth: Penguin).
G. Sanctuary and C. Whitehead (1976) *Divorce and After* (London: Oyez).
P. Willmott (1976) *A Consumer's Guide to the British Social Services* (Harmondsworth:
     Penguin).

Addresses
Cruse, National Widows' Association, 126 Sheen Road, Richmond, Surrey.
Gingerbread, 9 Poland Street, London NW1 – also for one-parent families.
Good Housekeeping Institute, Chestergate House, Vauxhall Bridge Road, London
     SW1V 1HF.
Family Planning Association, 27 Mortimer Street, London W1.
National Children's Bureau, 8 Wakley Street, London EC1.
National Council for One Parent Families, 255 Kentish Town Road, London NW5.
National Marriage Guidance Council, Herbert Gray College, Little Church St., Rugby
     CV21 3AP.
National Women's Aid Federation, 51 Chalcot Road, London NW1.
Pregnancy Advisory Service, 58 Petty France, London SW1.
Prisoners' Wives Service, 373a Brixton Road, London SW9 7DE.

RIGHTS

Books and materials
A large number of information leaflets on many aspects of rights can be gathered during a short tour of the local post office and branch of the Department of Health and Social Security. It is essential to do this from time to time as details of administration, amounts of various benefits, and other factors are altered as time goes by. However, you can get an overall picture of the rights area by having a look at some of the following:

Equal Rights (1976; set of information leaflets; London: ILEA Learning Materials Service).

L. Grant, P. Hewitt, C. Jackson, and H. Levenson (1978) *Civil Liberty: The NCCL Guide To Your Rights* (3rd edition; Harmondsworth: Penguin).

F. Greenoak (ed.) (1976, 1977) *What Right Have You Got? Your Rights and Responsibilities as a Citizen* (London: BBC Publications): a well-illustrated accompaniment to a radio series.

P. Hodge (1976) *Legal Rights* (London: Arrow Books).

R. Irving and C. Anthony (1976) *Know Your Rights: A Guide to Everyday Law* (Newton Abbot, Devon: David and Charles).

R. Lister (1976) *National Welfare Benefits Handbook* (6th edition; London: Child Poverty Action Group).

J. Mays, A. Forder, and O. Keidan (eds) (1975) *Penelope Hall's Social Services of England and Wales* (9th edition; London: Routledge and Kegan Paul).

P. O'Higgins (1975) *Workers' Rights* (London: Arrow Books/Society of Industrial Tutors).

L. Titchener and A. Winyard (1976) *Consumers' Rights* (London: Arrow Books).

C. Ward (1976) *How to Complain* (London: Pan).

P. Willmott (1976) *A Consumer's Guide to British Social Services* (Harmondsworth: Penguin).

Addresses
Advertising Standards Authority, 15–17 Ridgmount Street, London WC1E 7AW.
Age Concern, 60 Pitcairn Road, Mitcham, Surrey.
Child Poverty Action Group, 1 Macklin Street, London WC2.
Citizens Advice Bureau – local or via the National Citizens' Advice Bureau Council, 110 Drury Lane, London WC2.
Citizens Rights Office – as Child Poverty Action Group.
Commission for Racial Equality, Elliot House, 10–12 Allington Street, London SW1.
Consumers' Association, 14 Buckingham Street, London WC2.
National Council for Civil Liberties, 186 Kings Cross Road, London WC1.

Office of Fair Trading, Field House, Breams Buildings, London EC4.

'Ombudsman', Office of the Parliamentary Commissioner and Health Service Commissioners, Church House, Great Smith Street, London SW1.

VIOLENCE

Books and materials

A. Bandura (1977) *Aggression: A Social Learning Analysis* (Hemel Hempstead, Hertfordshire: Prentice-Hall).

J. Boyle (1977) *A Sense of Freedom* (London: Pan).

T. Gill and A. Coote (1977) *Battered Women* (London: National Council for Social Liberties).

R. W. Novaco (1975) *Anger Control* (Lexington, Massachusetts: Lexington Books).

E. Pizzey (1974) *Scream Quietly or the Neighbours Will Hear* (Harmondsworth: Penguin).

L. Taylor (ed.) (1973) *Violence Sociopack* (London: Sociopack Publications).

H. Toch (1972) *Violent Men: An Inquiry into the Psychology of Violence* (Harmondsworth: Penguin).

N. Tutt (ed.) (1976) *Violence* (London: HMSO).

Addresses

Criminal Injuries Compensation Board, 10–12 Russell Square, London WC1.

National Association for the Care and Resettlement of Offenders, 125 Kennington Park Road, London SE11.

National Society for the Prevention of Cruelty to Children, 1 Riding House Street, London W1P 8AA.

ALCOHOL − AND OTHER DRUGS

Books and materials

T. Cook, D. Gath, and C. Hensman (eds) (1969) *The Drunkenness Offence* (Oxford: Pergamon).

Drugs, A Basic Guide (1978) and *Drugs and the Law* (1978) (London: Release Publications).

N. Kessel and H. Walton (1965) *Alcoholism* (Harmondsworth: Penguin).

P. Laurie (1965) *Drugs: Medical, Psychological, and Social Facts* (Harmondsworth: Penguin).

C. MacAndrew and R. B. Edgerton (1970) *Drunken Comportment: A Social Explanation* (Sunbury on Thames: Nelson).

W. R. Miller and R. F. Munoz (1976) *How to Control Your Drinking* (Englewood Cliffs, New Jersey: Prentice-Hall).

The Non-Medical Use of Drugs: Interim Report of the Canadian Government Commission of Inquiry (1971; Harmondsworth: Penguin).

D. Robinson (1976) *From Drinking to Alcoholism: A Sociological Commentary* (New York: Wiley).

Royal College of Psychiatrists (in press) *Alcohol and Alcoholism: The Report of a Special Committee* (London: Tavistock).

C. E. Thoresen and A. McAlister (1976) *How to Become an Ex-smoker* (Englewood Cliffs, New Jersey: Prentice-Hall).

Addresses

Alcoholics Anonymous, P.O. Box 514, 11 Redcliffe Gardens, London SW10 – also has many local branches.

Alcoholics Recovery Project, 47 Addington Square, London SE5.

Institute for the Study of Drug Dependence, Kingsbury House, 3 Blackburn Road, London NW6.

National Council on Alcoholism, 45 Great Peter Street, London SW1P 3LT.

Release, 1 Elgin Avenue, London W9.

OTHER ADDRESSES

The Open University, Walton Hall, Milton Keynes MK7 6AA.

Workers' Educational Association (Central Office), 9 Upper Berkeley St., London W1.

8 Applications

It is often said, in tones of increasing resignation, that people from different disciplines speak fundamentally different languages. This is held to be true whether the disciplines in question are those of work or of the academic. The apparent exaggeration is not wholly unjustified, especially when we look at the fields of education and social work. Students of many academic subjects pick up textbooks and discover that there are different 'perspectives' to be brought to bear on any problem, but in practice learn to think in terms of one, and only one, of these. Often their final marks will be awarded according to the extent to which they have adopted this perspective to the exclusion of others. Similarly, professionals in many areas of work learn only about the methods employed by their profession – usually exclusive of other methods which might be just as useful. Although what they learn may contain considerable variety in itself, it often remains hopelessly narrow compared to the range of methods that might be employed. The effect of the adopting of particular perspectives, of attachment to particular methods, and of acceptance – frequently unarticulated – of assumptions adhering to either of these, inevitably is to create an impression of groups that speak different languages, heading for different destinations by mutually invisible routes.

This language 'barrier', if we can call it that, has a number of effects. The commonest of these are the inevitable 'breakdowns in communication'. These derive in part from the fact that workers with different backgrounds of training have different perceptions of the goals towards which they are heading, and of the means of achieving them; and they can arise quite independently of bureaucratic and administrative 'barriers' which are responsible for so many other types of breakdown. They are derived more deeply, however, from the fact that people's lives do not divide themselves up obediently into the segments that government Ministries and theories of social work have created for them, and from the awkward truth that solutions to individual problems are not necessarily to be found by the reflex application of rote learning methods in one area, casework in another, and family therapy in the next. Yet workers and helpers in many areas have been trained to behave as if this were often the case; and they invariably have problems in understanding the mode of operation in the department down the road. A related consequence, of course, is disillusionment – disillusionment that so much time may need to be taken up in consultations with other professionals and, more seriously, that so many failures accrue, as is unavoidable when one method is applied to many different kinds of problem.

A related effect, and one which has been taking deeper root in recent years, has been a wider sense of disillusionment: that of the consumers of professional services with the services themselves. This has been articulated in some circles in calls for 'de-professionalization' – directed even at medicine, a hitherto hallowed precinct of professional self-consciousness. But its most common expression is to be found in the sullen hostility and suspicion that can exist between the consumers of the Welfare State and its agents: between pupils and teachers, clients and social workers, offenders and probation officers, and mental hospital patients and psychiatric staff. If there were viable alternatives to these services, many of them might well go out of business tomorrow; the success of many voluntary and self-help agencies is evidence of this.

People with problems on the other hand speak a common language: that of the problems themselves. They define them and, if possible, try to cope with them by any means at their disposal; and if provided with tools for understanding and solving their problems more effectively, which they themselves can recognize, will engage wholeheartedly in doing just that.

Chapter aims

This chapter is about ways of providing some of these tools: about the possibility of applying the approach outlined in this book to individuals' problems in whatever setting they arise, and about ways of doing this that dispense with the specialized language of one or another profession. The results of doing so will, hopefully, involve better relations between different kinds of worker, on the one hand, and between workers in general and the people they serve on the other. The overriding aim of this chapter is ambitious: to try to break down some of the barriers that are created during training, by suggesting the use of the present approach in a number of areas. But, in general, we should emphasize at the outset that these are not the only areas of possible application. We hope that workers in other areas will see potential applications for themselves: there appears to be no reason why this approach should not be used in *any area whatsoever*.

The detailed aims of this chapter are, therefore:

1 briefly to summarize the ways in which the approach has been used so far, and look at some of its effects in practice;
2 to outline and develop suggestions for its application in a number of problem areas, and illustrate these with some examples;
3 to look at some practical issues in the use of this approach;
4 to sketch out superficially some additional areas of possible application.

Previous work with the approach

This approach is based on actual experience. It has been developed from work with several hundred people, including: offenders in prisons and on probation, in homes and hostels, and in day centres and day training centres; intermediate treatment groups; alcoholics; psychiatric patients; and school leavers. In addition it has provided an approach to the training of a number of different kinds of staff, including prison officers, probation officers, social workers, residential workers, hostel staff, teachers, careers officers, occupational therapists, psychiatric nurses, and volunteers.

In developing the approach from work with these groups, the actual problems which have been touched on are almost too numerous to mention. A glance through these might be the best possible way of reinforcing the suggestion that the approach could be applied in almost any setting. They include:

- finding jobs and keeping them, finding out about training, etc.
- handling problems at work
- finding accommodation, handling difficulties that arise
- finding out about rights and learning how to obtain them
- developing social skills, learning about others
- finding out about oneself
- solving family problems, both practical and interpersonal
- handling drinking problems, planning recovery for alcoholics
- dealing with violence (in oneself and others)
- interacting with particular groups, e.g. police, opposite sex, officials
- taking tests and filling in forms
- finding information, making decisions, making plans, learning to think
- solving money problems, budgeting, handling debts, financial planning
- planning courses – for offenders, schoolchildren, or staff of many kinds
- doing research.

The actual number of specific problems that have arisen under each of these headings is extremely large; a moment's thought about any one of them (try brainstorming!) will give some idea of the variety of things that might appear. There is also a large number of more specific areas which have been considered in a more cursory fashion, such as problems with drugs, gambling, developing leisure interests, coping with changes of status, staff team building, organizing work, group problem solving, and learning to teach.

The amount of time that has been spent on different problem areas is, of course, disparate; some problems are much more ubiquitous – and pressing – than others.

The approach outlined in this handbook promises, then, two interrelated things: a way of working with people who have personal problems; and a systematic set of activities designed to help those people do something constructive about their problems. Working in this way demands a considerable investment of staff time and other scarce resources to prepare and implement programmes. Before committing themselves to this expenditure, agencies and workers will want some assurance that the expense will be justified by the results they can reasonably expect to achieve.

The approach should commend itself to users at the purely conceptual level, appealing as it does to everyday rationality and common sense, and advocating the adoption of a straightforward cycle of problem-solving methods. The 'conceptual' aspect of the approach was derived, however, from day-to-day work. The practice came first, and the 'theory' evolved out of it – not, as often happens, the other way round. And, because it is an essentially practical approach, the best way to test it is to do it. Our own findings from experience can be described in terms of general feasibility, staff performance, and participant response.

FEASIBILITY

Most of the constituent activities described in this handbook require no testimonials: they are fully developed methods with long histories of successful use in their own right. What this approach has tested is the particular combination of these methods into four stages of a problem-solving process – assessment, setting objectives, learning, and evaluation – and the assembly of programmes along these lines.

This configuration has been tried out on many occasions, in a great many situations, with a wide range of personal problems, and by a variety of staff personnel. Not one of these exercises has been terminated due to the inability of the staff to sustain the programme or the unwillingness of the group members to continue with it.

The programmes themselves have been organized as weekly evening sessions, as one- or two-day full-time exercises, and as continuous courses for anything up to eight weeks of full-time activity from 8 a.m. to 5 p.m.

STAFF PERFORMANCE

As far as we can see, so far there appear to be no limitations on who is capable of running problem-solving exercises of the sort we have been describing. Highly trained graduate social workers, students, non-professional social workers, residential staff, prison officers – all have organized and carried out programmes ranging from two or three days or weekly sessions, to courses lasting many weeks. As might be expected with such a diverse set of people, the results they have obtained have varied widely, from the near disastrous to the highly successful; but the general experience has been one that staff have enjoyed and found personally fruitful.

The 'training' undergone by these workers has varied from a six weeks' full-time course to half a day. Although such a short period of training is not desirable, some at least of the half-day graduates did extremely well. Again, though not ideal, staff who have grasped the basic ideas and have some confidence in their ability to put some of the methods into use are well able to learn 'on the job' actually running a programme and preparing themselves and their material from day to day or from session to session.

The numbers of staff involved in the programmes have also differed widely, from one person aided by outside speakers and specialists, to fifteen professionally qualified workers. The ratio of staff workers to participants has covered a range from 1:10 to 1:1, but an average would be 1:6. All these programmes have been organized for groups, some of them as small as three or four, some as large as twenty. There is no reason why the approach and some of the methods described should not be used with individuals; but the organization of such expensive facilities, if they are to be used economically or justifiably, would seem to call for groups.

GROUP MEMBERS' RESPONSES

The built-in evaluation stage of personal problem solving is not only useful to participants at the time and to staff who want to know how they are doing: it also yields a permanent and growing record of participant response to the approach. Several hundred evaluations tell, between them, a generally consistent story: one of success. Some of the things that people claim to have gained from the sessions or courses they have attended include:

enjoyment – good atmosphere, friendly, informal, freedom of speech
information – new things learned, new ideas, information about sources of help
learning about self – greater self-awareness and insight into motives
learning about others – working in groups, hearing about other people's experience, attitudes, and views, tackling common problems, tolerance of others
confidence – increased confidence in the ability to tackle personal problems, greater self-confidence in personal interaction
thinking straighter – being able to analyse problems, learning to reflect before acting

changed attitudes – towards self, towards others, towards officials at work, towards life in general

changed behaviour – improved communication skills, reading and writing better, getting on better with other people, no longer drinking, no longer gambling, handling aggression better, better family relationships.

One person might gain in anything from one to four or more of these areas. Some have gained nothing in any of them – but they are a remarkably small proportion of the total. It is not possible to say who is likely to benefit from this approach and who will not: it seems to have nothing to do with intelligence, personality, types of problem, or even with level of motivation. A sizable number of people have volunteered for courses without any serious intention of looking at their personal problems and doing anything about them. Many of them have become involved in the momentum of the activities and appear to have learned as much as those who arrived with impeccable motives. On the other hand, it has been found to be counter-productive to try to keep someone in a group who does not really wish to be there.

There is, of course, no guarantee that results like this can be achieved on every occasion with every group of participants. But there is enough evidence to suggest that good results are the rule and bad ones the exception. And, even in an otherwise disastrous experience, there always appears to be someone who has gained something from it. When everything comes out right – staff, group, programme activities, etc. – the result is a glimpse into a different order of things characterized by goodwill, good humour, and co-operation; and this has happened sufficiently frequently to dismiss the idea that its occurrence is some kind of social 'lightning flash'. The outcome seems to be more predictable than that.

But other people's results are like second-hand shoes: the comfort of a shoe has really to be proved by wearing a pair of your own. The bulk of this chapter is devoted, therefore, to an exploration of some areas in which similar results might be obtained, by suggesting some applications of this approach.

Areas of application

For the present we can look at the areas of application under four major headings:

1 *Transitions*, with particular reference to leaving institutions of some kind;
2 *Day-to-day work*, both inside and outside institutions, in a large number of different fields;
3 *'One-off' problems*: use of the approach or of particular methods for dealing with specific topics or problems;
4 *Staff training and course organization* in any of the above areas, and many more besides.

TRANSITIONS

The normal cycle of life involves transitions of many kinds: psychological and emotional, such as development into adolescence, maturity, and old age; social, such as marriage, divorce, changes of status at work, and so on; not to mention transitions that are associated with entry into, and exit from, a whole range of social institutions, some of which are experienced by us all, others of which we come across only as a result of particular events in our lives. Examples of such institutions are schools, community homes, colleges, hospitals, and prisons. Passage into and out of different phases of the life-cycle – of whatever kind – is all too often associated with difficulties for individuals. This is especially true of institutions whose alleged aim is to help us cope with the problems that are responsible for getting us there. Yet little is done systematically to furnish help with difficulties of this kind.

Though many institutions exist to control us, they can have a protective function too, in satisfying many of our immediate needs, and relieving us of the troublesome burden of having to think for ourselves. The case of the man about to leave prison is particularly illuminating in this respect. But such a transition, and the problems associated with it, is also to be found in many other places, for example:

- leaving school, particularly for those who will not be continuing education;
- discharge from hospital, particularly for short-stay psychiatric patients;
- exit from community homes, intermediate treatment centres, detention centres, truancy or 'disruptive pupil' centres; or
- departure from hostels of various kinds.

If the approach presented here were to be applied to these problems, its basic aims in each case would be fairly simple:

1 to equip users with the skills they need for coping with problems facing them on the other side of their 'transition';
2 to enable users to make independent plans associated with any area of their lives that they specify as requiring attention;
3 to develop, for staff members of the institution in question, sets of particular methods and resources for systematically meeting the above needs.

There are a number of ways in which this could be organized. First, there are full-time courses for whole groups of individuals at a time. While these inevitably require the development of more material and a greater deployment of staff time than any other mode of organization, their effectiveness is considerable, and they have the advantage that they can be planned as whole units from start to finish. Second, courses basically similar to these can be run but on a less than full-time basis, e.g. two days a week, two sessions a week, one evening session a week, or any other combination of hours that suits the people involved. Third, the entire programme could be organized simply as a series of individual sessions, with a staggered rather than a block intake, so that people could come along as they liked, according to what was going on. The last is the least satisfactory but does have the advantage that individuals can attend right up to their date of departure. (With a course of fixed length, people can be leaving at varying periods after its conclusion.)

A large number of factors are bound to influence what choice of course organization is made: the type of institution; the staff-to-user ratio; the availability of resources; and the existence of alternatives which may be in competition with the course meetings. Also of importance in this respect is the relation of this kind of activity to the rest of the institution – for example, the availability of longer-stay groups, as in prisons or psychiatric hospitals, who might be able and willing to help out. The possibility of involving such groups is something we shall be touching on again in the next section.

What kinds of problem could be dealt with in this manner? The actual specification of them would of course depend on the groups involved, but we can anticipate at least some of them for particular groups as follows:

- *for school-leavers*: finding work; going on to further education or training; the use of leisure time (or unemployed time); spending money; changed relationships with family; the opposite sex; possible plans for moving to another area; general self-awareness;

- *for young offenders leaving centres of various kinds*: again, finding work; rights; finding accommodation; managing money; relationships with peers, resisting group pressures; alcohol, other drugs, smoking; coping with stigma and related problems; interacting with police;

- *for short-term psychiatric patients*: coping with anxiety or depression; basic social skills; coping with work, accommodation problems, handling money; alcohol, drugs, smoking; self-awareness and self-esteem; relationships with family and friends; marriage problems;

- *for other specific problem groups* it should be possible to develop courses and modules suited to their specific needs: in this respect one thinks especially of alcoholics, violent offenders, football 'hooligans'; those convicted of vandalism or motor-car theft; and, on the receiving end of the problem, as it were, parents of children temporarily in care, families of truants, and so on.

While these problems are of course exceedingly diverse – and are only a sample of what would actually arise – they nevertheless have basic elements in common. Individuals need to know more about themselves and about their problems before they can cope with them: there are certain to be aspects of the problems that they can specify for change (i.e. their objectives); there will invariably be information they require, attitudes and feelings of concern to them, skills they could easily develop – if not all of these simultaneously; and their performance in doing any or all of these will certainly – in our experience at least – provide them either with solutions to their problems, or with fodder for a second, and more confident, attack on them. For each of these processes, some at least of the methods and materials described in Chapters 4 to 7 should prove useful.

But departure from a closed environment is not the only kind of transition to which the methods outlined in this book could usefully be applied. Still in the field of institutions, the whole problem of arrival and adjustment presents itself as one to which too little attention has been paid. Too often, individuals are committed to institutions of various kinds without being given a sufficiently complete picture of what they can obtain from it; their being placed in it is simply a stop-gap solution for society, which places such goals as their removal or separation from other people above all else. Long-term incarceration of offenders, or prolonged hospitalization of some psychiatric patients, are no solutions to the problems they are alleged to deal with; but, until we find better solutions, the problems of adjusting to such treatment, and of doing something as useful as possible with it, still have to be faced. The approach presented here could, with only minor adaptations, serve this purpose equally well: the problems, for example, of coming to terms with a life sentence, or organizing time and work within it, or at least attempting to make it as useful as possible to those who must endure it, could all be explored fruitfully using methods outlined in the preceding chapters.

Similarly, the process of dealing with transitions while they are in progress, or at least on a before-and-after basis, could be made easier using this approach. Thinking again of prisons, it would be worthwhile to explore the use of these methods for the organization of self-help after-care groups with links on both sides of the prison wall. The general model here is simply that of using a variety of methods to prepare for the transition (in this case, release) and following on later with other methods to enable individuals to monitor their progress, obtain extra help if necessary, and reinforce their knowledge, feelings, and skills with additional amounts of learning. Such a model could equally well be applied to discharge from hospital, with Community Health Councils or psychiatric social workers providing the follow-up. It might even be possible to organize courses *around* discharge or release, with the event itself in the middle.

Finally, many other kinds of transition suggest themselves, which are obvious sources of difficulty for individuals but which are denied any sources of help or organized, associated activity. One thinks, in this respect, of retirement from work, of preparation for particular jobs or roles, of the birth of the first child in a family, and of the married woman's return to work after child-bearing. Thinking of these and planning something around them would require great inventiveness, but some of the methods described here might provide a starting-point for some suitably motivated person.

DAY-TO-DAY WORK IN THE FIELD OR INSTITUTION

Perhaps the vast proportion of individuals' problems are not, however, related to changes in degrees of freedom, status, or role, but simply arise in the course of ordinary living – they simply 'come up' as the result of particular events or sets of circumstances. Though many of these will be dealt with by individuals themselves, possibly with help from their families, many others involve recourse to one or other of the helping agencies – the social services, or voluntary charitable organizations.

An approach to problem solving, and a framework for organizing an almost unlimited pool of useful activities, such as that outlined in this book, could have a large number of applications here. We can look at these under two principal headings: first, possible applications by field workers of various kinds; and, second, uses of the approach for the internal organization of a number of different kinds of institution.

A number of exercises have already been carried out by probation officers working in the field, and there is no reason why similar exercises should not be attempted by workers in many areas, dealing with a very wide range of problems. Experiments that have been tried include, for example, a one-week block exercise for young unemployed probationers in the area of job search and decisions about work, and a series of ten weekly sessions for a group of offenders with drug-related problems, looking at the hurdles of decision-making in relation to work and spare time. Extensions of such applications could be envisaged in numerous directions, including looking at other problem areas, at uses by other kinds of field worker, and at various modes of organizing and actually implementing the methods chosen.

For example, field workers in numerous areas of the social services might envisage applying this approach to different 'interest groups' amongst the people they work with. By an 'interest group' we mean simply a group of people with a common problem, who could benefit a great deal by simply being in contact with each other, and benefit even more were this contact cast in the form of group problem solving or learning of some kind. The apparent violation of the principle of confidentiality that might be thought to take place here is of course no problem as long as individuals are invited to take part – the choice of whether or not to do so is theirs and the degree of self-disclosure involved is each individual's own decision. Thus interest groups might be formed out of individuals in the job market, around the area of job search, as mentioned above, or from individuals on the dole who are simply looking for better ways of spending their time – perhaps as a means of keeping out of trouble (in the case of young offenders), perhaps to achieve some particular objective, or perhaps simply for its own sake. Interest groups could be composed of individuals from one area, looking at the problems of the area in general, as in community development work; or they might comprise individuals with particular problems such as accommodation, drinking, drugs, debts, social skills, anxiety, or family difficulties of various kinds. They could contain individuals with the same overall difficulties, such as unmarried mothers or other single parents, parents of mentally-handicapped children, or elderly people living on their own. Finally, they could be groups with some shared objective as a whole, such as looking at a particular community problem (e.g. racial discrimination in the area), pressurizing an official body into action of some kind, or setting up some amenities for the community in which they live.

What this would mean for a field social worker would depend on what exactly he tried to do, and with which kind of group or problem area; but in general it requires little more than a reorganization of the use of time. People with problems of a specific nature – let us say family difficulties, for example – are contacted and asked, if they are interested, to come along to an introductory meeting at an arranged time and place. If the general outline of the problem is presented as the users would see it, there should be no difficulty in recruiting a suitable group. The group so formed can then pursue its interests, holding meetings at the same time, for two hours, every week for as long as they wish. Their activities could consist of assessment, setting objectives, learning, and evaluation tailored to the particular topic being dealt with. Alternatively, a more formal course could be advertised, setting out some of the activities to be engaged in, and perhaps including provision for one or two speakers or visits to places thought to be relevant. The evolution of the latter, more formal approach might in fact depend on some 'pilot' work with a less structured group, to explore typical problems and develop ways of dealing with them; but even the most formal group of this kind should allow a considerable amount of freedom to participants in designing later parts of the 'course' for themselves. In this way it can be fashioned more carefully to meet their needs.

This is just one variation amongst many, and it would be an error to underestimate some of the practical difficulties that would be encountered, such as finding space and so on and, for certain kinds of group, finding enough interested individuals. The answer to the latter problem may lie in a pooling of 'case loads' between two or more workers – a process that affords the additional advantage of involving more staff. Generally, were social workers to add this dimension to their work (and, of course, some have done so on such topics as welfare rights, etc.), there seems little doubt that the quality of service which they would be able to give would increase enormously, not to mention the increased satisfaction they themselves would experience. There is little doubt, as well, that it would be a more efficient way of working: that running several informal courses in parallel with different interest groups would enable staff to reach more individuals, more effectively, more often. Indeed, once many of these courses had been set up, they could more or less run themselves.

Many social workers do run groups, of course, and we should say here that what we are suggesting is not simply using groupwork *per se*, or having series of group discussions, or encounter groups, or people dropping in together for cups of tea. We are advocating the implementation of the methods surveyed in this book: the use of self-assessment materials and techniques; the setting of personal objectives by group members; the provision of opportunities for them to meet those objectives; and evaluation of the effects and of the process as a whole.

If the notion of weekly meetings between individuals with a common problem does not appeal, there are many other ways of implementing the approach: more general courses for mixed groups covering a variety of topics; solid weeks of intensive work with specific kinds of problem; or, simply (and we shall expand on this below), using some of the techniques on their own with particular individuals. The possibilities are manifold, and depend mainly on the will and enthusiasm of the workers involved.

Working along similar lines, staff of many institutions could organize at least part of their activities in one or more of these ways. Asking residents of institutions to participate in two-hour problem-solving sessions, once a week, or in more formal exercises lasting one to five days, would receive a welcoming response in many such places where the day has little structure in other respects. This could provide part of the work activities (or at least an option) in many community homes, in many wards and special units of psychiatric hospitals, in intermediate treatment centres, in probation homes and hostels, and even in schools as part of the curriculum usually taken up with 'liberal studies', 'social education', 'civics', or whatever it happens to be called in your particular establishment. The focus again would simply be on personal problem solving: on exploring individual problem areas, specifying goals, and investigating ways of dealing with the problems, and acquiring skills for doing the same in the future. Again, for particular groups with difficulties in readily identifiable areas – such as social skills deficits, finding and using information, or handling drinking problems – there is a host of useful exercises which can be arranged into a programme for that particular group. Workers in such institutions could readily prepare a programme or package from which their residents could derive great benefit – and many of the latter would be only too happy to help in developing such programmes themselves.

To sum up: the process of applying the approach outlined in this book to continuing work with individuals' problems is broadly similar both in institutions and in the field. The same kinds of problem exist in both areas; and, though in actual detail and in day-to-day working there are differences, none of them would invalidate the use of these methods. Workers who decide to implement the approach are faced with a small number of basic questions which have to be answered.

1 *Is the area of application in the field or in an institution?*

In the field as:
social worker?
probation officer?
psychiatric social worker?
community development worker?
careers officer?
youth worker?

In an institution such as:
school?
community home?
borstal?
psychiatric hospital?
probation home?
hostel?

2 *Would the course that is planned be:*

general, looking at a mixed bag of problems?
specific, dealing with one problem area for one group only?
something in between?

3 *What would be the scale of the course?*

Length:
a week?
a month?
ten weeks?
one year?

Frequency of meetings:
full-time daily?
one day a week?
two one-hour sessions per week?
one three-hour session fortnightly?

4 *How structured would the content be?*

highly, with a pre-arranged programme of activities, speakers, etc.?
unstructured, dependent on suggestions of group members?
something in between?

The varied answers that might be given to these questions may illustrate the flexibility of the approach; if workers in different areas can answer these questions and emerge with the basic outline of a programme in their heads, they are already half-way to implementing it.

ONE-OFF PROBLEMS

Earlier in this book we emphasized the principle of 'plagiarism', of acquiring and making use (within the limits of the law) of any methods or materials that appeared useful in helping individuals solve their problems. It would be surly to suggest that anything other than this principle should also apply to the contents of this book as a whole. *Any* specific technique, *any* idea, applicable to *any* problem, mentioned *any-where* within the covers of this work (and we hope elsewhere) should be seen by prospective problem solvers as there for the taking. In order to make use of these methods, it is not necessary to mount a course, have regular meetings, or work in groups. Their application (which is widespread in any case) can follow almost any pattern that users think useful. Thus, putting together an information-search exercise for a class of school leavers, but using nothing more, is still to be highly recommended. Working with a single individual on a single problem – even with yourself on a problem of your own – is still worth a try. Using a single assessment tool, a single method of setting objectives, a one-off learning device, or an isolated evaluation technique are all admissible as ways of applying what is here. There are no property rights on the materials in this book (unless cited in the sources): they are in common ownership and, for every kind of technique that exists, you can concoct your own version, and launch it on the world.

STAFF TRAINING

As described earlier, one major application that has been made so far of the approach outlined in this book is the training of staff, who in their turn would implement the approach in a variety of areas, including prisons, day training centres, hospitals, schools, hostels, social work, and probation. The organization of these courses was a close parallel – indeed an analogue – of the courses which trainees themselves would run, introducing each aspect of the approach much as it has been introduced in this book, and asking course members actually to try methods themselves at every stage. What has emerged is a formula for staff training, a mode of working that builds on the strengths of the individual, while introducing him (or her) to as wide a range of resources as possible. It is only a short step from this to the suggestion that the approach can also be used as a method for training staff in many areas, for designing training courses, and for furnishing a great deal of the content of these courses. Perhaps the most remarkable consequence of using the approach for this purpose is that some very simple tools – notably the learning matrix presented in Chapter 7 – provide individuals with keys for organizing their thinking, allowing them access to methods and materials from an extensive range of sources, and enabling them to identify areas of deficit which they can subsequently make good.

A major force in this respect is the principle – enunciated in full in Chapter 2 – of *optimism*: that on training courses, as elsewhere, high expectations are rewarded by high-level achievement. This is not to advocate pressurizing people into hard work – though much of this can be hard work (while rarely seeming like it) – but simply to emphasize once again that a fairly open set of expectations that individuals are capable of far more than they normally envisage usually contributes to their achieving just that. In our experience, performance is more heavily influenced by expectations than by anything else.

Users of this approach could probably design and run their own staff training courses. Previous courses along these lines have lasted from two days to six weeks. Obviously, the more time the better; but a great deal can be imparted in two days, and much of the learning of how to apply the methods described here takes place while actually putting them into practice. Given even the briefest taste, many individuals will continue on their own.

This book could also be used as an instructor's manual for running courses on the approach. The major innovation that would have to be made would be in emphasizing that, at each stage, rather than telling people about methods or materials, it is best to let them try some for themselves. This can be done by examining values, by sampling in succession different methods from each of the four stages (both in terms of doing them oneself and designing new strains of them), by setting programme construction exercises for course members' own areas of working, and by feeding back discussion and evaluation of all the results. Once people have tried this approach in practice, they are usually able to run courses on it themselves.

By way of summary, then, let us simply reiterate that the reflexiveness of the present approach is such that it can itself be used as a means of training people to implement it in practice.

Practical issues

The foregoing has suggested some of the more obvious applications of 'social skills and personal problem solving'; workers in specific areas will doubtless think of many more. But it would be idle to suggest that there are no problems in putting these verbal conjurings into effect. The present section tries to illuminate the slightly darker side of the process as a whole.

(1) If the organization of this book has given the impression that using this approach is a relatively smooth-flowing business, we had best dispel the illusion immediately: it is messy. As presented here, the process is already something of an abstraction. While at every stage there is an abundant supply of things to do, in practice the choice of these, their application to the highly individual perception of problems that can emerge, coupled with the inevitable vagaries of working with groups and individuals, combine to ensure that the progression will be different every time. On the other hand, the same variability provides some of the excitement and novelty of using the approach. The experience of approaching problems and developing the means of solving them can be at times bewildering, at times exhilarating. Its outcome is certainly unpredictable: there are sufficient sources of variation to ensure that the process never happens in the same way twice.

(2) A problem that accompanies this, if the approach is being used with groups, is the relative imbalance of attention focussed on individuals on the one hand, and the group as a whole on the other. It is often very difficult to spend sufficient amounts of time working with individuals by themselves; the activities – and often the atmosphere – of groups demand a disproportionate amount of one's interests. One possible solution to this problem might be to incorporate a lot of peer interviews, or general working in pairs, into the programme; another is to have staff teams always working in pairs (at least), with one conducting work with individuals that has been timetabled into the programme. (Alternatively, you can simply work with individuals.) In general, however, it is very difficult to get this right: it is a natural tension intrinsic to the process, which most of the time does no damage anyway, but which may, occasionally, have somewhat disruptive effects.

(3) Another inevitable problem is one that emerges from the principle of plagiarism. While there are many resources, methods, and materials that are available to everyone, and many others that can be developed by the users themselves, there are a small number of items that are for restricted usage. The most obvious of these are some psychological tests. However, in most areas, there will be psychologists working in some neighbouring agency – a university, polytechnic, hospital, education department, or whatever – who will probably be very happy to administer and score tests for interested groups. Tests themselves do, of course, cost money, and it might be necessary to budget for this in looking at resources in general. Another item that is restricted in availability, because of its cost, is video equipment, and other audiovisual aids (though cheaper) may also be hard to find. Again, however, these can be borrowed or hired: many schools, colleges, and polytechnics have video equipment lying unused in some department or other, which they will often make available for needful groups.

(4) A rather more deeply rooted problem that may sometimes emerge in applying this approach is that it occasionally conflicts with other styles of working. This is so in two senses. First, organizing a course programme or learning curriculum, speaking to groups, making contacts with other agencies – carrying on many of the activities essential to problem solving and many others (such as role-play) which are part of social skills training – could be said to involve something of an extrovert approach to working with people. Those who are accustomed to one-to-one working may feel that the prospect of addressing a group of twelve individuals is a bit daunting. The best answer to this is simply to use the approach with individuals, or with groups small enough to be manageable – say, two or three members.

A second sense in which there may be a conflict of styles is the more professional difficulty that may arise because of accepted ways of working in different kinds of establishment. It might cause serious argument if professionals in any one area were suddenly to abandon the cherished work-habits of their colleagues. In fact, however, there is an admixture of styles of working in most fields, to some extent: often very limited, but sometimes quite considerable. Also, the approach of this book suggests using any method that is available, and there is no reason why, on a day-to-day basis, this approach should conflict with anything else. The problem might arise when assumptions of particular ways of working come to be questioned: then, arguments might ensue; until such problems arise there is no way of saying exactly how they might appear.

(5) The final set of problems that can arise in practice do not really apply to this approach more than to any other. Problems about the constitution and management of groups, about whether or not so-and-so's video equipment is available on the day you want it, or about whether or not something is clearly explained, can all arise regardless of how you are working. Most of them can be overcome by careful organization; others will never be anticipated however thorough your preparation.

Some other applications

A final, brief aim of the present chapter is to make reference – inevitably in a superficial way – to some other potential uses of the approach. None of these have as yet been tried. Some demand a considerable effort of the imagination. But on the face of things there seems no reason why the methods outlined here should not be just as useful as those currently in use in numerous areas. They could include:

- group problem solving by management teams in industrial or bureaucratic organizations
- negotiation and conciliation processes, between unions and employers, and between countries
- organizing learning of any academic or technical subject, or designing courses associated with these
- pastoral counselling in schools
- planning work organization in autonomous working groups, self-help groups, and communes
- helping people to slim or stop smoking
- teaching thinking skills, helping to develop creativity, boosting intelligence
- designing new towns or other communities with the help of their future residents
- developing new methods for use in any of the above, or any other area that suggests itself.

This sounds ambitious, readers may say; but all of these things have to be done, and some of them are not being done too well at present.

Illustrations

To help make the central portions of this chapter more useful, some outlines of possible uses are given below, drawn from a variety of areas. Again, it has to be stressed that these are only some of the possibilities; users will undoubtedly be able to think of many more, and develop their own programmes for working.

Illustration 1 PROBLEMS OF FINDING AND KEEPING WORK: A ONE-WEEK FULL-TIME COURSE FOR OFFENDERS ON PROBATION

Day	Session 1	Session 2	Session 3	Session 4
Monday	Introductions Discussion Outline	Introduce video Let group see themselves	Write job histories Peer interview: 'job I liked'	Self-assessment with 'seven-point plan' Review and group discussion
Tuesday	Connolly Occupational Interests Questionnaire* + results	Saleable skills form Peer interview: 'job I'd like to get'	Brainstorming session: good and bad aspects of work	Differential Aptitude Tests: mechanical, verbal Review discussion
Wednesday	Why work? Form and discussion	Speaker from Jobcentre: 'training opportunities'	Feedback test scores Setting personal objectives: ladders + wall sheets	Peer interviews/ fishbowl discussion on personal goals Review discussion
Thursday	Speaker from F.E. College, Skillcentre, firm, or Careers Office, etc.	Job search simulation: job description, letter of application, use of telephone	Simulation continued: role-plays of interviews, + video	End of simulation Discussion: of job search, of sources of information Review discussion
Friday	Playback of video Self-rating exercises Looking at strengths and weaknesses	Structured role-plays: problems at work + discussion	General review of goals Long-term planning of goals Summary of week	Brief evaluative session

Notes Course members would be provided with personal files.
Numbers: up to fifteen or sixteen with two members of staff; up to eight or ten with one.
Provision of additional facilities to include:
    – leaflets, etc., on job information
    – optional individual sessions with counsellor
    (booked, e.g., for one afternoon)
    – optional films on specific jobs, or visits to local workplaces.
* Available from the Careers Research and Advisory Centre (CRAC), Bateman St., Cambridge.

Illustration 2 DECISION-MAKING COURSE FOR SCHOOL-LEAVERS: TWO SESSIONS (ONE-AND-A-HALF HOURS EACH) PER WEEK FOR ONE TERM OF TWELVE WEEKS

Week	Session 1	Session 2
1	Introduction to the course Outline of contents Opportunity for suggestions by pupils	Self-assessment: what plans do individuals have? what are their strengths and weaknesses? Peer interviews
2	Completion of check list (specially prepared) of school-leaver problems + discussion	Review of main contents of course: job search, managing money, spare time, personal relations
3	Work assessment: interests and abilities, spare-time jobs, parents' work	Work assessment: why do people work? Group starts a survey of reasons for working
4	Money problems: pocket money and wages/future income – how is it to be spent?	Money problems: looking at the prices of things that group members want to spend their money on
5	Spare time: how people spend it, diary forms Peer interviews on 'best and worst weeks of my life'	Spare time: answering some basic questions about how people in the group spend their time: alone, at home, purposefully, etc.
6	Personal relationships: self-assessment of 'the people who are important to me' Check list of problems	What kinds of relationships do people have with each other? Group devises its own typology Discussion of typical problems
7	Thinking about goals in the four areas Ladders + wall-sheet exercises	Discussion on goals in areas of course Asking group members to specify one other area for a 'project'
8	Job search simulation: job advertisements, applications, interviews	Job search simulation (cont.) Video recordings, if available
9	A speaker from outside on careers opportunities Questions and discussion	Money game: 'win as much as you can' Speaker or film on 'ways of making money go further'
10	Spare time: class members give talks on one way they will spend their time after leaving school	Personal relationships: speaker or teacher on birth control, VD, and sexual relationships
11	Project time: working in teams on a project in an area of importance to the group	Project time (cont.)
12	Groups present projects Discussion	Looking back at personal 'dossiers' Thinking about long-term goals Discussion Evaluation of the course

Illustration 3 COURSE ON FAMILY PROBLEMS: ONE SESSION OF ONE-AND-A-HALF
HOURS FOR TEN WEEKS FOR USERS OF THE SOCIAL SERVICES

Session	Contents
1	Introduction to the course and personal introductions 'Icebreaker' game, e.g. Broken Squares Group brainstorming of problem areas
2	Family problem check list (specially prepared), or general check list with a section on family problems Sentence-completion exercises Peer interviews: describing the inside of your home, or a member of your family
3	Pattern notes on individual problems Introduction of a problem-solving system Assessing personal strengths: ten best points exercise set for next week
4	Video of best points + playback Personal perception forms: 'as I am'; 'as family members 1, 2, . . . see me'; 'as I would like to be (or be seen)' Discussion
5	Diary forms: when do problems arise? '5W-H' on problems Form subgroups to work on specific areas, e.g. money, conflict, parenting, sex Assess problems in subgroups
6	Drawing together assessment material Identifying changes that can be made: check lists; sentence completion; wall sheets; peer interviews Formation of group contracts
7	Sources of help: speaker on marriage guidance or other area of interest to the group
8	Critical incidents analysis of conflicts at home Generate incidents; role-play; model and rehearse alternatives Set goals for next week: to handle just one incident better (group members specify possibilities)
9	Co-counselling session Group members analyse problems presented by each other and generate possible solutions Force-field analysis of suggestions
10	Review and evaluation session Looking at changes in situations or in attitudes Level of achievement of subgoals

Note This would be suitable for up to ten people with one or two course organizers. If more were known about the problems of individuals in advance, they might set themselves 'homework' each week, consisting of simple goals they wish to achieve, and review their progress at the end. Division into subgroups would only be necessary if individuals' problems were diverse in nature: a group could be formed with a single common problem.

Illustration 4 STAFF DEVELOPMENT: TWO SESSIONS AIMED AT DEVELOPING STAFF ORGANIZATION IN A VOLUNTARY CENTRE OF SOME KIND (MAINLY USING ASSESSMENT AND OBJECTIVE-SETTING TECHNIQUES)

Session 1

Introduction to the purpose of the group
Personal introduction
Sentence completion: 'I want to work here because . . .
Saleable skills form *and/or* skills survey
Peer interview on previous experience related to the work
Group discussion

Session 2

Learning Styles Inventory or other cognitive-style assessment method
Group discussion on patterns that may be emerging
Composition of large sheets listing skills and strengths of group members, compiled by *other* group members; comparison with individual's self-assessments
Relationship of these to aims of organization
Team-building and objective-setting exercise: 'This team needs . . .'; 'I can supply . . .' (possibly using sociometric choices for various roles)
Collation of all personal data and decisions about staff organization
Group discussion and review

References

R. Barnitt, D. Flegg, V. Hemsley, J. McGuire, P. Priestley, and D. Welham (1977) Prisoners and Prison Officers – A New Relationship? An Experimental Approach to Pre-release Preparation, in, *Research Bulletin No. 4* (London: Home Office Research Unit, HMSO).

B. Commons *et al.* (1978) Release Courses – A New Role for Prison Officers, *Prison Service Journal*, April.

P. Hardwick (1977) Discharged with Confidence, *Community Care*, 2 November.

M. Phillips (1977) Warders and Inmates Can Be Pals, *Guardian*, 5 December.

P. Priestley and J. McGuire (1977) Preparing Prisoners for Release, paper at State of the Prisons Conference, University of Kent at Canterbury, June.

9   The staff role

During the discussion of values it was suggested that the relationship between group members and group organizers was not that of teacher and pupils, but a partnership in trying to solve personal problems. Having reviewed some of the activities that can be used to try to achieve this goal, it may be helpful to say something more about what might be expected of someone who decides to work in this way with other people. There are a number of basic skills which have to be mastered and not a little information to be acquired. There is also the matter of personal style and the values that lie behind it, both of which seem to have a bearing on how the job gets done.

There is not, however, any one way of doing these things which is any more correct or likely to be rewarded with success than any other. Successful staff members appear to have little in common beyond the results they obtain in their work. The message seems to be: be yourself and concentrate on helping group members to do all the hard work for themselves.

Basic skills

The ability to talk to other people is probably the most important of all the skills required to run a competent problem-solving programme. But this does not mean the silver tongue of the salesman or the considered profundity of the therapist. It means rather the ability to ask good questions and to make sensible responses, and to have the capacity for listening to what others say. Additionally, the staff member should be able to encourage others to talk freely, and to listen to one another. These qualities can be summarized as interviewing skills and group leading skills.

INTERVIEWING

Considering the pervasive presence of interviewing in everyday life, and its fundamental importance, it is curious how little attention is ordinarily devoted to becoming skilled in it. On the other hand it is equally curious to observe the song-and-dance that is made about the art of interviewing by some of those who make a living out of it. Interviewing is essential in problem solving for several reasons:

1 It is a basic tool for collecting information about people and their problems, and the solutions to them. Interviews can be conducted by experts, staff members, and fellow group members to find out about all sorts of things: for instance, attitudes, aptitudes, or ambitions.
2 It is a necessary part of the recruitment process to give applicants an idea of what they will be doing, and to form a preliminary idea of the problems they may wish to work on.
3 It is a basic problem-solving technique which should be passed on to group members as a take-away asset for future use.
4 It is the medium within which all counselling takes place.

Interview formats have been considered in the assessment chapter but there are one or two rules which it may be helpful to have in mind when approaching the task of interviewing.

1 Listen to what the person being interviewed is saying. This may seem obvious, but many interviewers appear to be bored by the proceedings, so look alert and follow the conversation. Listening also implies not talking too much. In assessment, the interviewer should not be talking for more than about 10 per cent of the time; the remaining 90 per cent should come from the person being interviewed.
2 Be courteous, another self-evident rule that is not always observed. This means treating interviewees with respect. One good way of doing this is to treat interviewees as though they were slightly more intelligent, slightly older, possibly of the opposite sex, and of slightly higher social status than yourself. None of this may be true, but it can work wonders in the way you come across to others – unless, of course, you encounter someone who actually fulfils all these conditions: the best thing to do in those circumstances is to try to treat such a person as an equal.
3 Be confident. You may not be to start off with, but it will come with practice. Nervous and unconfident interviewers produce nervy and unconfident interviewees, so relax. You are not on show and are just doing your job to the best of your ability.

GROUP LEADING

Leading a discussion is rather like conducting a multichannel interview. Most of the comments made above hold good for both activities. But there are also some features of groups that require special attention. They are not the mysterious and complex entities they are sometimes made out to be, but they do sometimes need careful handling.

Leading a group discussion during a problem-solving exercise is, however, different from running an encounter group. For a start, group discussion should always have a clear purpose that can be explained in simple terms to everyone who is taking part, e.g.

'This discussion is intended to look at ways of locating jobs', or
'We shall now discuss our experience of drawing Supplementary Benefits'.

This straightforward approach does not, of course, rule out discussion of deeper or more personal things such as attitudes to women or to sexual morality, or the way in which people see themselves and others; but even on emotionally loaded topics the intention is to have a reasoned discussion about them. It is no part of this process to provoke expressions of extreme emotion which may cause distress to the individual and embarrassment to the group. Deeply felt issues will almost certainly arise in the ordinary business of discussing what goes wrong in people's lives, and there is no need to go looking for them. And if the conversation is kept purposeful and polite it is unlikely that anyone will be hurt by it.

At the same time it is not possible to predict and control everything that goes on in groups: antagonisms may suddenly flare up; there will be alternating periods of elation and depression which have no apparent cause and no obvious cure. But handling these does not depend on long previous training or a grasp of long words from groupwork literature. Dealing with these crises effectively is something that comes with experience.

The principal purpose of group discussion is to assist in the learning process: learning from the experience of others; finding out other people's views; and exploring ideas in more depth and with more breadth than is possible by introspection alone. Group leaders do not need exceptional powers to achieve these common-sense ends, just a sense of purpose, a plan of action, concern for the feelings of everyone present, and an ability to keep discussion going for as long as seems useful.

TEACHING

Teaching is, in turn, an extension of group leading. Where, in an interview, a sentence or two will suffice to define the purpose of the exercise, a group discussion may require a short presentation from the leader of some facts, opinions, or questions that will stimulate the conversation. Teaching simply means stretching that kind of contribution into a slightly longer and more varied form. Not too much longer, because the tolerance of a human being for listening to the speech of another is strictly limited, and teaching should not, therefore, be confused with 'lecturing'. Teaching is the presentation of materials in ways that are the most appropriate for the learning task in hand. This could mean giving a five-minute talk, but it also means introducing a film or a pencil-and-paper exercise, distributing a hand-out, organizing projects, running a role-play or a simulation, or anything else that seems a good idea at the time. Some simple rules about direct teaching are:

1 Be prepared. After a while you can stand up and talk about almost anything with hardly any forethought. But to begin with it is a good idea to plan what you are going to say and, if necessary, to write most of it down and learn it by heart. If the facts or ideas you are putting across are interesting, relevant, and accurate it will not matter too much if the performance falls slightly short of BBC standards. Performance will improve in time, but in the first place it is the content that is important.
2 Practice what you are going to say: in front of the mirror, in the car as you drive to work, or under your breath in the bus queue.
3 Look at the audience when you are talking. This may be difficult at first, but try to look at everyone you are speaking to at least once, and more often if possible.
4 Relax and try a joke or two. Nothing is so serious that some humour will not help it along.
5 Move about, vary the speed and pitch of your speech, and keep the whole thing as short as is realistic for the material you are presenting. Five minutes is long enough to speak on anything continuously, followed by discussion or some other activity, followed by another five minutes of talking, and so on.

After a few attempts most people become quite proficient at presenting information to groups of people. The same is true of video-tape recorders, overhead projectors, film projectors, slides, audio-tapes, hand-outs, etc.; a few minutes' practice with each is all that is usually necessary to master machines and other teaching media.

ADMINISTERING TESTS

This is another area where the professionals have tended to make things appear more difficult than they need be. There are some very complex psychological tests which demand considerable understanding of theory and technique and of mathematical processes for scoring purposes. But there are a great many simpler measures which can be administered by lesser intellects after even the briefest preparation. A clear idea of the purpose of any pencil-and-paper exercise is the most important thing the tester must communicate to the person who intends to do it. This purpose can often be written down in a sentence or two and learned parrot fashion if need be. For example:

> 'The aim of this problem check list is to enable people to pick out personal problems that are of concern to them, and to indicate how seriously they are affected by them.'

When group members have grasped the purpose of a test and agreed to try it for themselves, all that remains to be done is to explain as clearly as possible the procedure for filling it in. Sometimes it is best to do a worked example on a wall sheet or blackboard and to ask for questions to make sure that everyone has got the idea. It is also a good idea to wander round while the form is being filled in to make sure that nobody is doing it completely the wrong way: someone usually is.

If a test produces self-evident results, then discussion can follow immediately on its completion. If it needs to be scored, this should preferably be done by the group members themselves, and then discussed. With only a little experience it becomes possible to administer pencil-and-paper exercises in such a way as to be interesting and fruitful for most of the individuals who do them.

WRITING PROGRAMMES

This has already been described in detail in Chapter 7. But it is important to repeat here that almost anybody who will give time and thought to the matter can produce respectable, usable programmes of their own. These may rely heavily on ready-made materials procured wholesale from other sources and put together in a way that is adapted to the needs of the group involved. Others may be much more original, containing exercises and games invented and tested by the organizers of the programme. There is room for the display of originality and creativity in both these models of programme building. The most typical programme will contain a nice balance of tried-and-tested methods and new materials on trial.

'Writing', in the programme sense, may mean nothing more than pasting extracts from a magazine article onto a sheet, xeroxing it, and using it as a hand-out on some topic. It may, on the other hand, involve several colleagues working together for long periods to produce role-plays or simulations of some aspect of the real world in which problems arise. Either or both of these things can be done by anybody who chooses to do them. They can be done well or badly; but nothing will survive as programme content unless it passes the stern test of use with people confronted with the problems of real life.

ORGANIZING

Some people do not see themselves as organizers, and will shy away from what appears to be the organizational complexity of some of the ways of working we have described. It is true that running something like a one-week job-search programme will be hard work the first time, because all the material has to be collected from scratch: all of the contacts for space and the use of resources such as video or film projectors have to be made; speakers must be secured; members must be recruited – and all against a background of nervous tension in case the whole thing is a monumental failure. But the second time around sees all these problems solved with an ease and absence of fuss that removes all thought of them as hard work. Assembling supplies of paperwork is harder the first time than ever it will be subsequently; recruiting members is an adventure at the start, but soon becomes routine. And yet familiarity will never bring boredom: no group is ever the same as the last, and every piece of material, however well worn, retains a predictable capacity to evoke the unexpected. If you or members of the group are ever bored, in the end there is only yourself to blame. You have to try very hard to bore people on the subject of themselves, their problems, and what they want to do about them.

Attitudes and values

We have stressed throughout this book the importance of respect for individuals and groups. This need not be maintained, however, with straight-faced piety: some of the most successful organizers mediate their concern for others by means of a robust irreverence. To some observers their working style might appear to be rude and inconsiderate, but they remain on good terms with those they appear to be abusing and treating with such scant respect. Groups of men working together are prone to adopt this manner with each other: direct, forceful, and funny. It is unwise to simulate this style if it is not what comes naturally, but it makes a change from the sepulchral scenes that characterize some ways of working with people.

At the same time there are equally successful programme organizers who are reserved to the point of introversion. The important thing seems to be to work in the way that suits you best and to adapt the curriculum to that. There is almost always a resident extrovert in a group who will enliven the proceedings. It is not necessary, in other words, to dominate a group in order to provide a genuine learning environment for its members. Nor is it necessary to exceed them in intelligence, wisdom, experience, or maturity. Expertise of all sorts will come with experience of running problem-solving groups, but the essence of it all is to stimulate the members to do their own learning in their own way.

The bus driver does not need to tower over his passengers in moral stature in order to deliver them safely to their destinations. He just has to do his job. The same is true of staff members who use this approach. Although what they do may sometimes appear, from the outside at least, to be highly structuring and directive, the balance of power remains firmly tilted at all times in favour of the users of the methods. Staff may draw lines on a piece of paper, but the group members fill the spaces between them with their own thoughts, feelings, and experiences; the group members set and, we hope, achieve their own learning targets; and, at the end of the day, if all goes well it is the group members who solve their own problems. The role of the staff member in all this is the modest one of aiding and seconding the efforts of the problem solvers.

And, finally, the staff member is generous with his skill and knowledge and know-how. Whatever he has he shares with group members. If he is skilled in interview technique, he passes it on as best he can. If he knows how to find out things, he teaches others to do the same. And in return he learns from them about things beyond his own experience.

References

Abercrombie, M. L. J. (1969) *The Anatomy of Judgement*. Harmondsworth: Penguin.
—— (1970) *Aims and Techniques of Group Teaching*. London: Society for Research into Higher Education.
Adams, C., Gagg, S., and Tayar, G. (1973) *Living Decisions in Family and Community* (Vol. 1). London: BBC Publications.
—— (1974) *Living Decisions in Family and Community* (Vol. 2). London: BBC Publications.
Adams, J., Hayes, J., and Hopson, B. (1977) *Transition: Understanding and Managing Personal Change*. London: Martin Robertson.
Allen, M. (1972) *The Save and Prosper Book of Money*. London: Dale/Collins.
Anastasi, A. (1976) *Psychological Testing* (4th edition). London: Collier-Macmillan.
Annual Careers Guide. London: Careers and Information Centre.
Argyle, M. (1967) *The Psychology of Interpersonal Behaviour*. Harmondsworth: Penguin.
—— (1973) *Social Interaction*. London: Tavistock.
—— (1975) *Bodily Communication*. London: Methuen.
Bailey, R. (1973) *The Squatters*. Harmondsworth: Penguin.
—— (1977) *The Homeless and the Empty Houses*. Harmondsworth: Penguin.
Bales, R. F. (1950) *Interaction Process Analysis: A Method for the Study of Small Groups*. Reading, Massachusetts: Addison-Wesley.
Bales, R. F. and Strodtbeck, F. L. (1968) Phases in Group Problem Solving. In, Cartwright, D. and Zander, A. (eds) *Group Dynamics*. London: Tavistock.
Bandura, A. (1963) *Social Learning and Personality Development*. New York: Holt, Rhinehart and Winston.
—— (1970) *Principles of Behaviour Modification*. London: Holt, Rhinehart and Winston.

—— (1977) *Aggression: A Social Learning Analysis*. Hemel Hempstead, Hertfordshire: Prentice-Hall.

Barnitt, R., Flegg, D., Hemsley, V., McGuire, J., Priestley, P., and Welham, D. (1977) Prisoners and Prison Officers – A New Relationship? An Experimental Approach to Pre-release Preparation. In, *Research Bulletin No. 4*. London: Home Office Research Unit, HMSO.

Bartlett, F. C. (1932) *Remembering*. Cambridge: Cambridge University Press.

Beauchamp, G. A. (1975) *Curriculum Theory* (3rd edition). Wilmette, Illinois: The Kagg Press.

Berne, E. (1970) *Games People Play*. Harmondsworth: Penguin.

Bingham, W. V., Moore, B. V., and Gustad, J. W. (1959) *How to Interview*. New York: Harper and Row.

Blamire, J. and Izzard, A. (1975) *Debt Counselling*. Birmingham: Birmingham Settlement Money Advice Centre.

Bloom, B. S. (1956) *Taxonomy of Educational Objectives: 1. Cognitive Domain*. New York: David McKay.

Bloom, B. S., Krathwohl, D. R., and Masia, B. B. (1964) *Taxonomy of Educational Objectives: 2. Affective Domain*. New York: David McKay.

Blumberg, A., and Golembiewski, R. T. (1976) *Learning and Change in Groups*. Harmondsworth: Penguin.

Bono, E. de (1971) *The Use of Lateral Thinking*. Harmondsworth: Penguin.

—— (1976) *Teaching Thinking*. London: Maurice Temple Smith.

Boyle, J. (1977) *A Sense of Freedom*. London: Pan.

Brody, S. R. (1976) *The Effectiveness of Sentencing*. Home Office Research Study No. 35. London: HMSO.

Bruner, J. (1966) *Towards a Theory of Instruction*. Cambridge, Massachusetts: Harvard University Press.

Bull, N. J. (1969) *Moral Judgement from Childhood to Adolescence*. London: Routledge and Kegan Paul.

Button, L. (1974) *Developmental Group Work with Adolescents*. London: University of London Press.

Buzan, T. (1974) *Use Your Head*. London: BBC Publications.

Carnegie, D. (1936) *How to Win Friends and Influence People*. New York: Simon and Schuster.

Cartwright, D., and Zander, A. (eds) (1968) *Group Dynamics*. London: Tavistock.

Cattell, R. B. (1965) *The Scientific Analysis of Personality*. Harmondsworth: Penguin.

Classification of Occupations and Directory of Occupational Titles (CODOT) (3 Vols.) (1972). London: HMSO.

Commons, B. *et al.* (1978) Release Courses – A New Role for Prison Officers. *Prison Service Journal*, April.

Cook, T., Gath, D. and Hensman, C. (eds) (1969) *The Drunkenness Offence.* Oxford: Pergamon.

Coote, A., and Gill, T. (1977) *Women's Rights, A Practical Guide.* Harmondsworth: Penguin.

Corsini, R. J. (1957) *Methods of Group Psychotherapy.* New York: McGraw-Hill.

Cronbach, L. J. (1970) *Essentials of Psychological Testing.* New York: Harper and Row.

Cross, C. P. (1974) *Interviewing and Communication in Social Work.* London: Routledge and Kegan Paul.

Directory of Projects (annual). Chichester: Barrie Rose.

Dominian, J. (1968) *Marital Breakdown.* Harmondsworth: Penguin.

Douglas, T. (1976) *Groupwork Practice.* London: Tavistock.

Drugs, A Basic Guide (1978). London: Release Publications.

Drugs and the Law (1978). London: Release Publications.

Equal Rights (1976) (set of information leaflets). London: ILEA Learning Materials Service.

Eysenck, H. J. (1953) *Uses and Abuses of Psychology.* Harmondsworth: Penguin.

—— (1962) *Know Your Own I.Q.* Harmondsworth: Penguin.

—— (1966) *Check Your Own I.Q.* Harmondsworth: Penguin.

Eysenck, H. J. and Wilson, G. (1976) *Know Your Own Personality.* Harmondsworth: Penguin.

Fair Deal – A Shopper's Guide (revised edition) (1978). London: Office of Fair Trading.

Falloon, I., Lindley, P., and McDonald, R. (1974) *Social Training: A Manual.* London: Psychological Treatment Section, Maudsley Hospital.

Flanders, R. G. (1976) *Type to Read with the New Dico System.* London: Dico Educational International.

Flowers, J. V. (1975) Simulation and Role-playing Methods. In Kanfer, F. H. and Goldstein, A. P. *Helping People Change.* Oxford: Pergamon.

Froebel, F. (1887) *The Education of Man.* Fairfield, New Jersey: Kelley.

Fry, E. (1963) *Teaching Machines and Programmed Instruction.* New York: McGraw-Hill.

Garrett, A. (1948) *Interviewing: Its Principles and Merits.* New York: Family Services Association of America.

Gibbs, G. I. (ed.) (1974) *Handbook of Games and Simulation Exercises.* London: E. and F. N. Spon.

Gill, T. and Coote, A. (1977) *Battered Women.* London: National Council for Civil Liberties.

Goldberg, M., Walker, D., and Robinson, J. (1977) Exploring the Task-Centred Casework Method. *Social Work Today* **9** (2), 6 September.

Goldstein, A. P., Sprafkin, R. P., and Gershaw, N. J. (1976) *Skill Training for Community Living.* Oxford: Pergamon.

Golzen, G., and Plumbley, P. (1971) *Changing Your Job*. London: Kogan Page.

Goodman, P. (1971) *Compulsory Miseducation*. Harmondsworth: Penguin.

Grant, L., Hewitt, P., Jackson, C., and Levenson, H. (1978) *Civil Liberty: The NCCL Guide to Your Rights*. Harmondsworth: Penguin.

Greenberg, I. A. (1974) *Psychodrama: Theory and Therapy*. London: Souvenir Press.

Greenoak, F. (ed.) (1976) *What Right Have You Got? Your Rights and Responsibilities as a Citizen* (Part 1). London: BBC Publications.

—— (ed.) (1977) *What Right Have You Got? Your Rights and Responsibilities as a Citizen* (Part 2). London: BBC Publications.

Gundray, E. A. (1975) *Making Ends Meet: A Practical Guide to Family Finance*. London: Arrow Books.

Hannam, C. (1976) *Parents and Mentally Handicapped Children*. Harmondsworth: Penguin/MIND.

Hardwick, P. (1977) Discharged with Confidence. *Community Care*, 2 November.

Hare, A. P., Borgatta, E. F., and Bales, R. F. (1966) *Small Groups: Studies in Social Interaction*. New York: Alfred Knopf.

Harris, T. (1973) *I'm O.K., You're O.K.* (London: Cape).

Heimler, E. (1975) *Survival in Society*. London: Weidenfeld and Nicolson.

Herbert, M. (1976) *Problems of Childhood*. London: Corgi Books.

Heavy Goods Vehicle Driver's Manual: A Guide to the Driving Test (1972) Bristol: Educational Services Ltd.

Higham, T. M. (1971) *Your First Interview*. London: Cornmarket.

Hodge, P. (1976) *Legal Rights*. London: Arrow Books.

Holt, J. (1976) *Instead of Education*. Harmondsworth: Penguin.

Hopson, B. and C. (1973) *Twosome Plus: A Guide to Cohabitation with Exercises*. London: Blond and Briggs.

Hopson, B. and Hough, P. (1973) *Exercises in Personal and Career Development*. Cambridge: Careers Research and Advisory Centre (CRAC).

Hopson, B. (1977) Personal Re-evaluation: A Method for Individual Goal Setting. In, Adams, J., Hayes, J., and Hopson, B. *Transition: Understanding and Managing Personal Change*. London: Martin Robertson.

Howe, A. and Romiszowski, A. J. (annual) *APLET Yearbook of Educational and Instructional Technology*. London: Kogan Page.

Hutten, J. M. (1977) *Short Term Contracts in Social Work*. London: Routledge and Kegan Paul.

Illich, I. (1970) *Deschooling Society*. Harmondsworth: Penguin.

Inbar, M. and Stoll, C. S. (1972) *Simulation and Gaming in Social Science*. New York: The Free Press.

Irving, R. and Anthony, C. (1976) *Know Your Rights: A Guide to Everyday Law*. Newton Abbot, Devon: David and Charles.

Jackson, K. (1975) *The Art of Solving Problems*. London: Heinemann.

Jeanneau, J. A. (1973) *Small Business Management: Instructor's Manual* (Vols. 1–5). Prince Albert, Saskatchewan: Training, Research and Development Section, Department of Manpower and Immigration.

Jehu, D. (1967) *Learning Theory and Social Work*. London: Routledge and Kegan Paul.

Johnson, D. W. and Johnson, F. P. (1975) *Joining Together: Group Theory and Group Skills*. Englewood Cliffs, New Jersey: Prentice-Hall.

Johnson, R. B. and Johnson, S. R. (1975) *Towards Individualized Learning: Developer's Guide to Self-instruction*. London: Addison-Wesley.

Jones, M. (1968) *Social Psychiatry in Practice*. Harmondsworth: Penguin.

Jongeward, D. and James, M. (1973) *Winning with People: Group Exercises in Transactional Analysis*. London: Addison-Wesley.

Jourard, S. M. (1963) An Exploratory Study of Body-Accessibility. *British Journal of Social and Clinical Psychology* **5**: 221–31.

Kanfer, F. H. and Phillips, J. S. (1970) *Learning Foundations of Behavior Therapy*. New York: Wiley.

Kanfer, F. H. and Goldstein, A. P. (1975) *Helping People Change: A Textbook of Methods*. Oxford: Pergamon.

Kerlinger, F. N. (1964) *Foundations of Behavioral Research*. New York: Holt, Rhinehart and Winston.

Kessel, N. and Walton, H. (1965) *Alcoholism*. Harmondsworth: Penguin.

Kinnersley, P. (1973) *The Hazards of Work: How to Fight Them*. Worker's Handbook No. 1. London: Pluto Press.

Klein, J. (1966) *Working with Groups*. London: Hutchinson.

Kolb, D. A., Rubin, I. M. and McIntyre, J. (1974) *Organizational Psychology: An Experiential Approach*. Englewood Cliffs, New Jersey: Prentice-Hall.

Korving, J. and M. and Keeley, M. (1975) *Out of the Rut*. London: BBC Publications.

Laufer, M. (1976) *Adolescent Disturbance and Breakdown*. Harmondsworth: Penguin.

Laurie, P. (1965) *Drugs: Medical, Psychological, and Social Facts*. Harmondsworth: Penguin.

—— (1976) *On the Dole: Your Guide to Unemployment Benefit and Other Things You Need to Know*. London: Kogan Page.

Lees, R. (1975) *Research Strategies for Social Welfare*. London: Routledge and Kegan Paul.

Lewis, H. R. and Streitfeld, H. S. (1970) *Growth Games*. London: Souvenir Press.

Lister, R. (1976) *National Welfare Benefits Handbook*. London: Child Poverty Action Group.

Longley, C. (ed.) (1975) *Adult Literacy Handbook*. London: BBC Publications.

Lynes, T. (1975) *Penguin Guide to Supplementary Benefits* (3rd edition). Harmondsworth: Penguin.

MacAndrew, C. and Edgerton, R. B. (1970) *Drunken Comportment: A Social Explanation*. Sunbury on Thames: Nelson.

Mackinnon, B. and Falsenfield, N. (1971) *Group Counselling and Psychotherapy with Adolescents*. New York: Columbia University Press.

MacMillan, P. and Powell, L. (1973) *An Induction Course for Teaching in Education and Industry*. London: Pitman Publishing.

McPhail, P. (1972) *In Other People's Shoes*. Harlow: Longman.

Mager, R. F. (1972) *Goal Analysis*. Belmont, California: Fearon.

Mays, J., Forder, A., and Keidan, O. (eds) (1975) *Penelope Hall's Social Services of England and Wales* (9th edition). London: Routledge and Kegan Paul.

Meichenbaum, D. (1977) *Cognitive Behavior Modification: An Integrative Approach*. New York: Plenum.

Miles, M. B. (1971) *Learning to Work in Groups*. New York: Teachers College Press, Columbia University.

Miller, R. (1978) *Equal Opportunities – A Careers Guide for Women and Men* (5th edition). Harmondsworth: Penguin.

Miller, W. R. and Munoz, R. F. (1976) *How to Control your Drinking*. Englewood Cliffs, New Jersey: Prentice-Hall.

Moorhead, C. (1975) *Helping – a Guide to Voluntary Work*. London: Macdonald and Jane's.

Mullen, E. J. and Dumpson, J. R. (1972) *Evaluation of Social Intervention*. San Francisco: Jossey-Bass.

Murray, M. (1975) *The Videotape Book*. New York: Bantam Books.

Neill, A. S. (1968) *Summerhill*. Harmondsworth: Penguin.

Non-Medical Use of Drugs: Interim Report of the Canadian Government Commission of Inquiry, The (1971) Harmondsworth: Penguin.

Novaco, R. W. (1975) *Anger Control*. Lexington, Massachusetts: Lexington Books.

O'Higgins, P. (1975) *Workers' Rights*. London: Arrow Books/Society of Industrial Tutors.

Oppenheim, A. N. (1968) *Questionnaire Design and Attitude Measurement*. London: Heinemann.

Opportunities for School Leavers (Vols. 1–4: published annually). London: New Opportunities Press.

Perls, F., Hefferline, R., and Goodman, P. (1973) *Gestalt Therapy*. Harmondsworth: Penguin.

Pfieffer, J. W. and Jones, J. E. (1970) *A Handbook of Structured Experiences for Human Relations Training*. Iowa City, Iowa: University Associates Press.

Phillips, M. (1977) Warders and Inmates Can Be Pals. *Guardian*, 5 December.

Pizzey, E. (1974) *Scream Quietly or the Neighbours will Hear*. Harmondsworth: Penguin.

Polanyi, M. (1958) *Personal Knowledge*. London: Routledge and Kegan Paul.

Priestley, P. and McGuire, J. (1977) Preparing Prisoners for Release. Paper at State of the Prisons Conference. University of Kent at Canterbury, June.

Rackham, N. and Morgan, T. (1977) *Behaviour Analysis in Training*. Maidenhead, Berkshire: McGraw-Hill.

Ravetz, J. R. (1971) *Scientific Knowledge and its Social Problems*. Oxford: Oxford University Press.

Reid, W. J. and Epstein, L. (1972) *Task Centered Casework*. New York: Columbia University Press.

Rennie, J., Lunzer, E. A., and Williams, W. T. (1974) *Social Education: An Experiment in Four Secondary Schools*. Schools Council Working Paper 51. London: Evans/Methuen Educational.

Robinson, D. (1976) *From Drinking to Alcoholism: A Sociological Commentary*. New York: Wiley.

Rodger, A. (1974) *Seven Point Plan*. London: N.F.E.R.

Rogers, C. (1965) *Client Centered Therapy*. London: Constable.

—— (1969) *Freedom to Learn*. Columbus, Ohio: Merrill.

—— (1973) *Encounter Groups*. Harmondsworth: Penguin.

Rose, S. D. (1977) *Group Therapy – A Behavioural Approach*. Hemel Hempstead, Hertfordshire: Prentice-Hall.

Rousseau, J.-J. (1762) *Emile*. London: Dent, 1974.

Royal College of Psychiatrists (in press) *Alcohol and Alcoholism: The Report of a Special Committee*. London: Tavistock.

Rudinger, E. (ed.) (1975) *How to Sue in the County Court*. London: Consumers' Association.

—— (ed.) (1976) *Dismissal, Redundancy and Job Hunting*. London: Consumers' Association.

—— (ed.) (1976) *Getting a Divorce*. London: Consumers' Association.

Rutter, M. L. (1975) *Helping Troubled Children*. Harmondsworth: Penguin.

Sanctuary, G. and Whitehead, C. (1976) *Divorce and After*. London: Oyez.

Sarason, I. (1968) Verbal Learning, Modelling, and Juvenile Delinquency. *American Psychologist* **23**: 254–66.

Sarason, I. and Ganzer, V. J. (1973) Modelling and Group Discussion in the Rehabilitation of Juvenile Delinquents. *Journal of Counselling Psychology* **20**: 442–49.

Saskatchewan Newstart (1972) *Socanic Coaching Manual*. Prince Albert, Saskatchewan: Department of Manpower and Immigration.

—— (1973) *Life Skills Coaching Manual*. Prince Albert, Saskatchewan: Department of Manpower and Immigration.

Schutz, W. C. (1973) *Joy*. Harmondsworth: Penguin.

Schweinitz, E. and K. de (1962) *Interviewing in the Social Services: An Introduction*. London: NCSS.

Sharpe, R. and Lewis, D. (1977) *The Success Factor*. London: Pan.

Shaw, J. (1973) *Basic Counselling*. Stockport, Cheshire: Vernon Scott Associates.

Sidney, E, and Brown, M. (1961) *The Skills of Interviewing*. London: Tavistock.

Sidney, E., Brown, M., and Argyle, M. (1973) *Skills with People*. London: Hutchinson.

Sperry, L., Mickelson, D. J., and Hunsacker, P. L. (1977) *You Can Make It Happen (A Guide to Self-Actualization and Organizational Change)*. Reading, Massachusetts: Addison-Wesley.

Spivack, G., Platt, J. J., and Shure, M. B. (1976) *The Problem-Solving Approach to Adjustment*. San Francisco: Jossey-Bass.

Supplementary Benefits Handbook (periodically revised). London: HMSO.

Taylor, J. and Walford, R. (1972) *Simulation in the Classroom*. Harmondsworth: Penguin.

Taylor, L. (ed.) (1973) *Violence Sociopack*. London: Sociopack Publications.

Taylor, L. C. (1972) *Resources for Learning*. Harmondsworth: Penguin.

Thoresen, C. E. and McAlister, A. (1976) *How to Become an Ex-smoker*. Englewood Cliffs, New Jersey: Prentice-Hall.

Tiffin, J. and McCormick, E. J. (1966) *Industrial Psychology*. London: George Allen and Unwin.

Titchener, L. and Winyard, A. (1976) *Consumers' Rights*. London: Arrow Books.

Toch, H. (1972) *Violent Men: An Inquiry into the Psychology of Violence*. Harmondsworth: Penguin.

Toch, H. (1977) *How to Survive Inflation*. London: Pitman Publishing.

Topham, T. (1975) *The Organized Worker*. London: Arrow Books/Society of Industrial Tutors.

Trower, P., Bryant, B., and Argyle, M. (1978) *Social Skills and Mental Health*. London: Methuen.

Tutt, N. (ed.) (1976) *Violence*. London: HMSO.

Vernon, P. E. (1969) *Personality Assessment: A Critical Survey*. London: Tavistock.

—— (1971) *Intelligence and Attainment Tests*. London: University of London Press.

Walker, N. (1957) *A Short History of Psychotherapy*. London: Routledge and Kegan Paul.

Ward, C. (1972) *Work*. 'Connexions' series. Harmondsworth: Penguin.

Ward, C. (1976) *How to Complain*. London: Pan.

Watkinson, D. and Reed, M. (1976) *Squatting, Trespass and Civil Liberties*. London: National Council for Civil Liberties.

Watts, A. G. (ed.) (1977) *Counselling at Work*. London: British Association for Counselling.

Whitfield, P. R. (1975) *Creativity in Industry*. Harmondsworth: Penguin.

Wilkins, L. T. (1967) *Social Policy, Action, and Research*. London: Tavistock.

Williams, A. (1975) *Educating the Consumer – A Practical Guide*. Harlow, Essex: Longman.

Willmott, P. (1976) *A Consumer's Guide to the British Social Services*. Harmondsworth: Penguin.

Wills, D. (1945) *The Barns Experiment*. London: George Allen and Unwin.

—— (1964) *Homer Lane*. London: George Allen and Unwin.

Zimbardo, P. G. *et al.* (1973) The Mind is a Formidable Jailer – A Pirandellian Prison. *The New York Times*, 8 April.

Zimbardo, P. G. (1977) *Shyness*. Reading, Massachusetts: Addison-Wesley.

Addresses

Advertising Standards Authority, 15–17 Ridgmount Street, London WC1E 7AW.

Advisory Service for Squatters, 2 St. Paul's Road, London N1.

Age Concern, 60 Pitcairn Road, Mitcham, Surrey.

Alcoholics Anonymous, P.O. Box 514, 11 Redcliffe Gardens, London SW10. (Also has many local branches.)

Alcoholics Recovery Project, 47 Addington Square, London SE5.

Birmingham Settlement Money Advice Centre, 318 Summer Lane, Birmingham B19 3RL.

Campaign for the Homeless and Rootless (CHAR), 27 Endell Street, London WC2.

Careers and Occupational Information Centre, 3 St. Andrews Place, London NW1.

Careers Research and Advisory Centre, Bateman Street, Cambridge.

Central Office of the Industrial Tribunals, 93 Ebury Bridge Road, London SW1W 8RE, and St. Andrew House, 141 West Nile Street, Glasgow G1 2RU.

Charity Commission, 14 Ryder Street, London SW1.

Child Poverty Action Group, 1 Macklin Street, London WC2.

Citizens Advice Bureau – local or via the National Citizens Advice Bureau Council, 110 Drury Lane, London WC2.

Citizens' Rights Office – *as* Child Poverty Action Group.

Commission for Racial Equality, Elliot House, 10–12 Allington Street, London SW1.

Consumers' Association, 14 Buckingham Street, London WC2.

Criminal Injuries Compensation Board, Russell Square House, Russell Square, London WC1.

Cruse, National Widows' Organisation, 126 Sheen Road, Richmond, Surrey.

Educational Services Ltd., St. Lawrence House, 29–31 Broad Street, Bristol.

Family Planning Association, 27 Mortimer Street, London W1.

Gamblers Anonymous, 17–23 Blantyre Street, London SW10.

Gingerbread, 9 Poland Street, London W1. (Also for one-parent families.)

Good Housekeeping Institute, Chestergate House, Vauxhall Bridge Road, London SW1V 1HF.

Hodder and Stoughton Ltd., P.O. Box 700, Mill Road, Dunton Green, Sevenoaks, Kent TN13 2YA.

Information Canada, Publications Satellite, P.O. Box 1565, Prince Albert, Saskatchewan S6V 5T2, Canada.

Inner London Education Authority, Learning Materials Service, Publishing Centre, Highbury Station Road, London N1 1SB.

Institute for the Study of Drug Dependence, Kingsbury House, 3 Blackburn Road, London NW6.

National Association for the Care and Resettlement of Offenders, 125 Kennington Park Road, London SE11.

The National Audio-Visual Aids Centre, 254 Belsize Road, London NW6.

National Children's Bureau, 8 Wakley Street, London EC1.

The National Committee for Audio-visual Aids in Education, 254–56 Belsize Park Road, London NW6.

National Council for Civil Liberties, 186 Kings Cross Road, London WC1.

National Council for One Parent Families, 255 Kentish Town Road, London NW5.

National Council of Social Service, 26 Bedford Square, London WC1B 3HU.

National Council on Alcoholism, 45 Great Peter Street, London SW1P 3LT.

National Federation of Consumer Groups, 61 Valentine Road, Birmingham B14 7AJ.

N.F.E.R. Publishing Company Ltd., 2 Jennings Buildings, Thames Avenue, Windsor, Berks. SL4 1QS.

National Institute of Careers Education and Counselling, Bateman Street, Cambridge CB2 1LZ.

National Marriage Guidance Council, Herbert Gray College, Little Church Street, Rugby CV21 3AP.

National Society for the Prevention of Cruelty to Children, 1 Riding House Street, London W1P 8AA.

National Women's Aid Federation, 51 Chalcot Road, London NW1.

New Opportunity Press, 76 St. James's Lane, London N10 3RD.

Office of Fair Trading, Field House, Breams Buildings, London EC4.

'Ombudsman', Office of the Parliamentary Commissioner and Health Service Commissioners, Church House, Great Smith Street, London SW1.

The Open University, Walton Hall, Milton Keynes MK7 6AA.

Pregnancy Advisory Service, 58 Petty France, London SW1.

Prisoners' Wives Service, 373a Brixton Road, London SW9 7DE.

Release, 1 Elgin Avenue, London W9.

Schools Council for Curriculum and Examinations, 160 Great Portland Street, London W1.

Shelter, National Campaign for the Homeless, 86 Strand, London WC2; Shelter Community Education Programme, 157 Waterloo Road, London SE1 8UU; and Shelter Housing Aid Centre, 189a Old Brompton Road, London SW10.

Small Firms Information Centres are available in each region of the country (in London, Luton, Bristol, Cardiff, Birmingham, Nottingham, Manchester, Leeds, Newcastle, and Glasgow); information can also be obtained from Small Firms Division, Department of Industry, Abell House, John Islip Street, London SW1P 4LN.

Society for Research in Higher Education, 25 Northampton Square, London EC1V 0HL.

Sociopak Publications Ltd., 2 Crawford Place, London W1H 1JD.

Trades Union Congress (TUC), Congress House, 23–8 Great Russell Street, London WC1.

Workers' Educational Association (Central Office), 9 Upper Berkeley Street, London W1.

Index